Boost Your Credit Score In 30 Days

Credit Repair Blueprint

Dana Robinson

COPYRIGHT © 2019 DANA ROBINSON
All rights reserved. No part of this publication may be reproduced, distributed, or transmitted in any form or by any means, including photocopying, recording or other electronic or mechanical methods, without the prior written permission of the publisher, except in the case of brief quotations embodied in critical reviews and certain other non-commercial uses permitted by copyright law. For permission requests, write to the publisher, addressed "Attention: Permissions Coordinator," at the address below.

Paperback ISBN: 978-1-79485-098-9

This publication is for informational purposes only and is not intended as legal advice. Every possible effort has been made in preparing and researching this material. We make no warranties concerning the accuracy, applicability of its contents, or any omissions.
First printing edition 2019.

http://www.bootoutcarbs.com
info@bootoutcarbs.com

TABLE OF CONTENTS

WHAT'S ON YOUR CREDIT REPORT?......6
WHAT IS IT? 6
   HOW TO BUILD GOOD CREDIT RIGHT FROM THE START 15
   HOW TO HANDLE YOUR FIRST CREDIT CARD 19
   HOW TO GET YOUR CREDIT REPORT 24
WHAT'S ON YOUR REPORT? 27
   UNDERSTANDING YOUR CREDIT REPORT AND SCORE 31
   MONITOR YOUR CREDIT REPORT 35
   SPOTTING IDENTITY THEFT 38
   HOW DOES IDENTITY THEFT AFFECT MY CREDIT?...41
   HOW TO PREVENT IDENTITY THEFT FROM HAPPENING TO YOU 44
WHY ARE THERE MISTAKES?...............48
   LOCATE THE CREDIT REPORT MISTAKES 49
TYPES OF CREDIT MISTAKES TO FIND.51
   INCORRECT ACCOUNT INFORMATION.....51
   OLD NOTATIONS ON ACCOUNTS............54
   MONITOR AND LIMIT INQUIRIES 57
   INQUIRIES...59
   IDENTITY MISTAKES 61
   HOW TO RESTORE YOUR CREDIT AFTER IDENTITY THEFT...................................63
TAKE IT STEP BY STEP 66
   IT TAKES TIME......................................68

TIPS FOR INCREASING YOUR CREDIT SCORE QUICKLY 70
CONTACTING THE CREDIT BUREAUS ... 80
   MAKING THE MOST OUT OF CLAIMS 81
   YOU'VE FOUND THE PROBLEM: NOW WHAT? 84
   GO TO THE RIGHT CREDIT BUREAU 89
HOW TO CLEAN IT UP 91
   THE BASICS OF CREDIT CLEAN UP 93
   CREDIT CLEAN UP: DISPUTE INCORRECT INFORMATION FROM YOUR CREDIT REPORT 97
   CREDIT CLEAN UP: PAYING OFF DEBT .. 100
   CREDIT CLEAN UP: MAKE A PLAN FOR THE FUTURE 103
   CHOOSING AND CREATING GOOD ACCOUNTS TO BOOST YOUR CREDIT 107
SAMPLE LETTERS: 112
   DISPUTE LETTERS 112
   ADDING POSITIVE ACCOUNTS 118
   DISPUTING INACCURATE INFORMATION AND/OR ERRORS 121
   DISPUTING INACCURATE INFORMATION AND/OR ERRORS 124
   DISPUTING NEGATIVE ITEMS AND/OR ERRORS 127
   DISPUTING NEGATIVE ITEMS AND/OR ERRORS 129
   DISPUTING ERRORS 132
   DISPUTING NEGATIVE ITEMS AND/OR ERRORS 135
   REMOVING INQUIRIES FROM YOUR CREDIT REPORT 138

    REQUESTING ORIGINAL CREDITOR TO
    INVESTIGATE A NEGATIVE LISTING 140
    GOODWILL LETTER 143
    REDUCTION OF DEBT 146
    DEBT VALIDATION LETTER - A SHORTER
    VERSION 150
BONUS TIPS 152
    PAY YOUR DEBT DOWN.......................152
    PAY MORE THAN MINIMUM PAYMENTS ..154
    PLANNING FOR A CREDIT-WORTHY FUTURE
   155
    LIVING WITHIN YOUR MEANS 156
    LIVE THE LIFESTYLE YOU CAN AFFORD .160
    USE CREDIT WISELY 161
    DON'T OVER OBTAIN..........................163
    DO USE CREDIT..................................165
    BUILD CREDIT WITH SECURED CREDIT
    CARDS 167
    DEBT NEGOTIATION: NEGOTIATE AWAY
    YOUR MEDICAL DEBT 169
    DEBT NEGOTIATION: CUT YOUR SCHOOL
    LOANS IN HALF OR MORE 173
    DEBT NEGOTIATION: TALK DOWN YOUR
    CREDIT CARD DEBT 177
    KNOW WHEN YOU NEED HELP 182
    HOW TO SPOT A CREDIT REPAIR SCAM 183

WHAT'S ON YOUR CREDIT REPORT?

Your credit report is an essential part of your day to day life, even if you may not realize it at first. Your credit report is used by credit lenders, home mortgage lenders, insurance companies, and even employers when each of them determines if they should, or should not, work with you. Do you know what is on your credit report? If not, there has never been a better time than right now to find out.

WHAT IS IT?

The first question that must be answered is the most important. What is your credit report? A credit report is a collection of information about you. This information is centered around your specific ability and experience with credit use. Credit, a form of money that is given to individuals to spend and repay over time, is given by lenders only if they believe you are a good risk to them. Every lender must define what level of risk is acceptable to them, but they base their decisions on the past usage of credit by you.

Let's explain. Over time, creditors lend to hundreds and thousands of people. They develop specific algorithms that help them define who is a credit risk by looking at the patterns in the way that individuals spend using credit. They determine how much risk they are willing to take to work with people. Risk is a calculated tool for lenders. The more risk you are, the more they can charge in the form of interest rates and fees. On the other hand, if there is too much risk from an individual, that individual is unlikely to repay their debts, and the lender stands to lose money instead of making it.

What does this mean for you, though? As a borrower, you need creditors to see you in the best light possible. The lenders to the credit reporting agencies directly report the decisions you make regarding credit.

- You obtain a credit card. You use it to make a $100 purchase. The credit card company reports this action to the credit bureaus, which keep track of all your activity.

- You make a payment on time to the lender. The lender lets the credit bureaus know. This looks good to them. Over time, regular payments increase your credit score.

- You make a late payment on the credit card. The lender reports this to the credit bureaus. This looks bad. Just one late payment will remain on your credit report for up to two years and can drop your credit score.

This record is kept ongoing from the time you first get some form of credit. The more good notches you get from your creditors, the better your credit score is. You may be wondering what a credit score is, too.

A credit score is a numerological representation of the credit report. The credit bureaus took all the information on you and put it into that complex algorithm to get a number that represents your credit usage. Credit scores can be under 350 up to 800, depending on the credit bureau. The higher the score is, the better. This shows the company that you are a good credit risk.

High credit scores mean:
- More lenders willing to give you credit
- Lower interest rates on new lines of credit
- More ability to borrow at a higher credit limit
- Lower interest rates possible on credit you already have

The key here is taking your credit score, no matter where it is right now, and improving it.

You can do this by understanding your credit report thoroughly and by making smart financial decisions going forward.

There is no instant credit eraser or improvement tool that works to move a 350 credit score up to 700. In fact, the credit bureaus will not tell you what percentage of improvement you will have if you make specific credit decisions. The fact is the mathematical formula they use is highly guarded. Instead, you will need several things to see improvement with your credit:

- Time
- Dedication to good credit usage
- Removal of any inaccurate information on your credit report

Also note that when creditors consider you for a credit card or loan, they most often use just your credit score, with a brief look at your credit report. Therefore, it is very important to do whatever it takes to get this number up.

Credit may seem like a trifle and fickle thing, but it can be demystified and used to help better your credit rating and score. Credit is when you borrow money against your own name to make payments on an item of high price or value. The highest forms of borrowing are often vehicles and homes, though jewelry, electronics, recreational vehicles, and many other items are available on credit, even furnishings and home goods can be bought on credit. With the expansion of credit over the past few decades, stores have cropped up their own store credit cards that you can use to purchase items in their stores and on their web sites on credit.

The positive of credit is the ability to finance something you cannot immediately afford and the option to build a solid credit rating, or name, for yourself for future borrowing power for the larger items like a house, which for 98% of people requires a loan. This borrowing power can also be extremely useful in the time of emergency when funds are low due to job loss, medical problems, injury, catastrophe, or the death of an income earner. Borrowing allows people to get through these tough times without sacrificing their quality of life.

The negative aspect of credit is that it has allowed people to live outside their means, and everyday millions of people find themselves further in debt. While this funds credit card companies, it can bring great hardship to those experiencing high levels of debt. Credit, when used wisely, can offer opportunities where there are none and help you find a greater level of borrowing in the future and help during a present situation, but when used unwisely can push you into a worse financial situation and negatively affect your future borrowing power.

When you turn eighteen, it seems that every bank and financial institution in the country suddenly has your personal information and wants to offer you "free money," this is a dangerous time, and you should avoid a good majority of these offers. It is wise to open one account, but only charge during a month what you can pay off completely before the due date. One or two open revolving accounts that are constantly in good standing offer a great way to build good credit. This can also be used when someone is bouncing back from bad credit or bankruptcy but can also be a slippery slope if you have not broken your bad spending habits.

Your credit report offers a reporting mechanism through three major agencies (Equifax, Experian, and TransUnion) that gather account, financial and personal information about you from the creditors and bills you have to form together a credit rating and thus a credit score that represents your ability to pay debt, your timeliness in paying your bills and how often you move or change jobs. While much of this information may not seem connected, it is all used to gauge whether you are a person worthy of credit, a job, or even renting an apartment. So, it's vitally important to set a good credit rating and practices from the start as credit impacts your entire life. Some bad credit and financial practices can lead to bankruptcy, which allows the debtor to wipe their debt clean, except for a few different areas (like school loans, taxes due and others) and start over. While this may seem like a dream to many, it sets you back and means you not only have a note on your credit report showing the bankruptcy and your inability to pay any of your bills but now you have essentially no credit and have to start over as if you were eighteen again.

Regardless of how you choose to handle your credit and your potential borrowing power, it's important to take the time to understand the credit rating and reporting process, not to mention the staying power they both have. Credit ratings, scores, and reports are essential to the quality of life and options available to individuals and can have a direct effect on your status or level of success throughout your life. Take the time to understand these things and work to set yourself up for better financial success.

HOW TO BUILD GOOD CREDIT RIGHT FROM THE START

Good credit is something that must be worked at and maintained. While it is difficult to rebuild good credit after financial stumbles, good credit from the start can be maintained much easier. The benefits of good credit can help you find the things you want earlier in life if you have the income to back it up. Being a smart consumer is part of how to handle your credit successfully. With a few tips and tricks, you can work at maintaining good credit right from your first account.

Tip #1: Only borrow exactly what you need. This is important because, frequently, people feel like they are getting free money, and they tend to borrow too much or overspend on credit and other store account cards. This can become a habit, and then before you know it you are in debt and on a slippery slope toward financial ruin and crippling debt. If you stick to only borrowing the amount you NEED, instead of what you WANT, you can save yourself money and hassle in the long run.

Tip #2: Choose your accounts and credit cards carefully. There are literally thousands of credit card companies out there, and almost every store offers a charge card or account of their own. It can be easy to fall into a life of charging and catch up if you aren't careful. Instead of sending out offers as soon as you get them, take the time to read the fine print and select only those with steady interest rates and from larger banks, because they tend to hold more weight on a credit report.

Tip #3: Only charge what you can pay back every month. Paying the minimum payment is a detrimental practice that leads to years of paying off one purchase. Instead, only charge exactly what you can pay in full each month. Not only is this easier on your finances, but it also reflects the best on your credit report by showing you pay your balances in full and on time.

Tip #4: Opt-out of excessive offers. Whenever you get a credit card or other credit offer in the mail, the company has already taken it upon themselves to pre-screen you, and this puts a negative mark on your credit report and can lower your credit score. Take the time to visit sites like donotmail.org or optoutprescreen.com to opt-out of future mailings and pre-screening.

Tip #5: Adopt smart spending habits and learn to live within your means. By doing these two simple things, you will learn how to and become habitual in smart financial practices, which in turn will positively affect your credit and credit score. Take the time to learn about smart financial practices and how to achieve the things you want in your life without going into debt to do it.

Regardless, of your level of wealth or responsibility when you turn eighteen or open your first credit account, you have the opportunity to start with a solid credit rating and maintain that throughout life to be able to access such things as home, vehicle and other important loans that many seek at some point in their lifetimes. Good credit, when properly maintained, can not only bring about ample borrowing situations and credit but can also offer you better employment, housing, and other opportunities.

Credit is used for a variety of things, and while borrowing and loans are the brunt's of the credit industry, many employers, landlords, schools, and other industries are using credit reports as a definition of character before deciding to work or not work with someone on what they desire. Good credit shows responsibility, awareness, and self-worth and can bring you more important things in life than just a nice house and a nice car. Take the time to learn about how to obtain and maintain good credit and find yourself with a richer life, some of which may have nothing to do with the money you have in the bank.

HOW TO HANDLE YOUR FIRST CREDIT CARD

Good credit is something that must be worked at and maintained. While it is difficult to rebuild good credit after financial stumbles, good credit from the start can be maintained much easier. When you turn eighteen, you will notice a barrage of credit card and other loan offers coming in the mail, calling you on the phone and popping up in your email. While some may be tempting with high limits and promises of low-interest rates and payments, these can be the traps that walk you straight into a large amount of suffocating credit card debt in the future.

To navigate through these offers, you should open them all and read ALL the information carefully. It's important to understand the information included with the offer. While they may be offering you 0% interest or some other enticing bit, the fine print will often reveal that the promotion is only for a short period or through certain restrictions. To help you decide which offers to pitch, which to keep and how to protect yourself from overwhelming numbers of offers, here are a few simple steps to follow.

1. Read the fine print.
As mentioned above, the fine print will often reveal loopholes in the promotions, time restrictions on your initial agreement, and other nasty little things, like fees for a variety of things and other negative surprises that

could jump out later down the line. If there is anything you are uncertain about or you find a company you are not familiar with, take the time to check them out with a site like ZapData or through the Better Business Bureau for complaints and in-depth information.

2. Consider the offers carefully to choose the right one for you.

Before you fill out, call or send off the credit card applications, e best fitted to your needs. This doesn't mean you should automatically pick the highest limit or lowest interest rate. As far as interest rates look for stability. If you are considering two different cards and companies and one offers 0% interest for the first three months, then the rate goes to 28%, is it better than a card that offers 8% interest and never changes? You want consistency with no surprises. As for the limit, picking the highest limit can be tempting, and you may end up making the card out and overspending

21

just because it's there. Instead, choose a card that offers a limit that can help you in an emergency but not high enough to get you in trouble.

3. Opt-out of future offers

When you selected the card or cards, you will apply for and use, it's important to take the time to opt-out of future offers and future mailings. The more offers you get, the more your credit is being checked and this is harmful to your credit score. You want to only allow the companies you ask to check your credit. There should be opt-out information on the application form itself, though it won't be readily available, you will have to look for it a little. Some organizations and sites can help you opt-out of the credit card offers without taking the time to contact each company separately. Check out donotmail.org or optoutprescreen.com for more information and to sign up.

4. Set some rules.

When you first get a credit card, it will seemingly burn a hole in your wallet. You will think about it all the time, and you will feel as if you have been given free money, especially if you live on a budget or fixed income and don't often have money for extras. Set some rules for yourself and follow some standard rules to avoid credit card debt. You should pay your balance every month and avoid paying the minimums. If you charge $1000 and only pay the minimum's, at an average interest rate, it would take you at least eight years to pay off the balance.

Credit cards can offer an emergency support system that you can fall back on in a time of financial hardship, but if not handled correctly can turn bad and land you in credit card debt that can be difficult to get out of.

HOW TO GET YOUR CREDIT REPORT

To obtain your credit report, you have several options. If you have never obtained a credit report in the past, or have not done so in the last 12 months, your first stop should be a visit to each of the three credit reporting companies:

- TransUnion: http://www.transunion.com/
- Equifax: http://www.equifax.com/home/
- Experian: http://www.experian.com/

Visit each company's website. There, you can request a free credit report. Recently, laws in the United States changed to require that each of the credit reporting agencies provide consumers with one free company of their credit report each year. The reason for this is that it is an estimate that more than 80 percent of credit reports have errors or missing information on them.

Think about what that means: 80 percent of people may be paying too much in interest, may not qualify for loans they deserve, or may even be turned down for a job because they have a poor credit score, through no fault of their own.

Once you get your credit report cleaned up, it is highly recommended that you invest the time in getting a free credit report at least one time per year from each of these companies to ensure that no errors are present. If you would like to avoid paying for additional credit reports, obtain a credit report from one of the credit bureaus every four months. This way, you do not have to pay for the credit report but get the latest information reported there.

Perhaps you have already obtained your credit report in the recent past. To get another one, you may need to pay for it. Most often, copies of your credit report are available for under

$20, though it may be slightly more if you would like to see your actual credit score.

You can purchase the credit report from each of the credit bureaus directly. Other companies are selling these but monitor the security and the overall cost. You may be able to get a credit report for much less if you go directly to the credit bureau for it.

The first time you obtain your credit report for the goal of cleaning it up, it is important to obtain a company of the report from each of the three credit bureaus. As mentioned earlier, later, you may not need to do this since most information will be the same from each of the lenders. Right now, you need to clean up the credit information on all three reports to ensure that your best foot is forward when it comes to credit usage.

WHAT'S ON YOUR REPORT?

Once you get to the credit bureaus, you will need to work through the questions they ask. This is important since it is verifying that you are the person you say you are. Once this process is complete, you will be taken to an online version of your credit report. You cannot change the information here directly but rather must go through a specific reporting process.

Before you get excited to see your information, you will want to look for specific information.

- Notice the number of accounts you have: The higher this number is, the more desperate you look to creditors. You do not want a high number.

- Notice any delinquent notices or collections notices on your report. These are some of the most damaging pieces of information listed on the report.

- Locate the credit card accounts listed. You may notice some that are very old, perhaps even your oldest credit cards. If they are good reports, for example, they are not reporting anything is in collections or overdue, leave them there! The longer you have had credit, the more experience you have. It is a good thing to have older cards, especially with good histories on your account. Do not remove these.

- Locate the inquiries listed. Inquiries are reported whenever someone requests to see your credit report. There are two types. Some come directly from credit card companies and lenders who you have requested credit from. These are the most important to notice since these work against your credit score. If you have too many inquiries listed, this could mean that you are again desperate for credit. It also drops your credit score. The second type is pre inquiries, where lenders are considering

28

offering you a line of credit. Since you have not requested credit from them, these types of inquiries do not count against you.

The credit report contains a wealth of information. Read through it and take notice of the individual accounts. You should notice each account listed, with information including the credit limit, the age of the account, the lender's name and information, and a few green (or other colored) boxes. Each month you have the credit account, this box will change in color or mentions. For example, you may notice a streak of green boxes. This means that you have made your payment on time those months, with one box representing one month. These boxes trail back for two years before they disappear.

Take some time to look through the credit report. Most of these reports are very easy to navigate, and they only take a few minutes to browse through. Each of the three credit agencies has also provided you with as much information as you need on the credit report. You may also find a section where the bureau is telling you why you have the marks you have, or the credit score you have.

They may give you specific information on how to improve the credit score, such as:

- Too many delinquent accounts: making payments on time helps to improve your credit score

- There are too many inquiries on your account

- There are too few credit card accounts open

This is specific information directed at you. Use this as a springboard telling you exactly what you need to do to see improvement in your credit score.

It is important to note that your credit report is only as good as what your creditors have reported. There are going to be errors on your credit report. Some will matter, some may not. The key here is to notice them and to take action to remove them. When you do this, you will find yourself with an improved report and potentially a higher credit score.

UNDERSTANDING YOUR CREDIT REPORT AND SCORE

Your credit score is based on a formulation used by the credit reporting agencies that create a general average of your credit history and assigns a number to show whether you have excellent, good, fair or poor credit. While your credit score is an average of your credit history, it is often the first thing creditors look at when deciding whether to give you a loan or credit account. While you are unable to change the credit score directly, you can change and better your overall credit and credit report, which will directly reflect on your credit score.

When looking for a way to improve your credit score, there are many steps in the process, and it will take a little bit of time for the improvements you make to reflect on your credit score. You can go through the process alone, or you can enlist the help of a credit counselor, which can help with the process, paperwork, and the law surrounding what you are allowed to change and dispute and what you are not.

Your credit report is available from each of the three major credit reporting agencies, including Experian, Equifax, and TransUnion. All these agencies have a web site where you can order your credit report that can be delivered in paper form or instantly electronically. Once you have your credit reports, print them out. This will take lots of paper, but it worth it to have them spread out in front of you for the best results when looking over them.

1- Know your credit

You may not know your current credit or have kept up with what is on your credit report until now. This is a big mistake. You should purchase, or get a free credit report, once a year to check for mistakes or fraud. If you never have, you will need to pay extra close attention to the items on your credit report.

2- Go through your credit report with a highlighter

Go through every part of your credit reports, including the personal information, highlight anything incorrect. This should include wrong addresses, name misspellings, accounts, and other items you don't recognize. Also, mark items that are yours but that you may dispute the balance, interest rate or other parts of the account.

3- Follow the directions for disputing inaccurate information

At the end of the printed and electronic credit reports are the instructions on how to dispute items on your credit report that you feel are inaccurate. You can complete this process in writing or online. When doing so, you will need to provide ample proof of the item you are disputing, whether that's receipts for an item you paid or proof of your identity to dispute an identity or past address problem. You should also always make copies of everything you send into the credit reporting agency.

Regardless of the information, you find on your credit report, it's important to understand how credit works and how you can improve and dispute the information on your credit report. The most important thing to take away from this is the need to get all three of your credit reports every single year to check for inaccurate information. This is not only smart financial practice but one of the best ways to protect yourself from identity fraud.

MONITOR YOUR CREDIT REPORT

As we have talked about, knowing what is on your credit report is the key to being successful at managing it. But, just pulling your credit report one time is simply not going to cut it. You need to know what is happening on your credit report regularly.

It is an option to get a copy of your credit report for free only one time per year from each of the three credit bureaus. This means that you can get a copy of your report every four months for free. Most of the time, the information included in one will be the same as all three reports. Nevertheless, there can be differences, which is where you need to be cautious.

If you have found very few mistakes on your credit report up to this point, do not worry about doing anything more than what you are already doing. If you are monitoring the report every four months, you should be all right, and you should catch errors often enough.

On the other hand, if you have a credit report that has been full of errors, especially those concerning identity theft or larger scale problems with address mistakes and problems with particular creditors, it is best to look for a service to help monitor your credit. These services are available through each of the credit reporting agencies, TransUnion, Equifax, and Experian.

There are a variety of types of service and reporting options to consider here. For example, you may choose to have just a copy of your credit report sent to you each month. You may want to watch your credit more closely and want to have a new report more often, such as every few weeks. You may want to know your credit score, too. The more often you need to know your credit report information, the more costly the reporting costs will be. The credit score is usually an additional cost to the credit report.

Reporting services like these can range in cost from $10 a month up to $30 or $40, depending on the type of service you select. Choose what works best for your individual needs. It may not be necessary to have a product that provides you with a large amount of information or frequent reporting unless you have been having significant problems.

SPOTTING IDENTITY THEFT

Mistakes can be more severe, though. There are plenty of situations where someone has obtained your personal information and is using it to get credit cards, loans, or even driver's licenses. This is called a stolen identity. While it may not seem like something that happens often, it does. In one report by USA Today, it is an estimate that one in four homes have a victim within it from identity theft.

Identity theft is one of the largest problems with credit bureaus today. There are countless cases of individuals struggling to take back their identity, too. The key here is for you to keep track of what is happening with your credit report so that you can report suspicious information to the proper authorities as soon as it becomes noticed. The sooner you spot the problem, the easier it is to remove it.

If you feel you have been the victim of identity theft, for virtually any reason, you should report this information to your local police. Most larger cities within the United States now have task forces capable of helping individuals with this type of problem specifically. The key is to get help as soon as you notice the problem.

Report the problem if you notice any of the following on your credit report, especially if more than one instance has occurred:

- You notice someone else's address or an address you have never lived at, especially out of state information
- You have multiple credit accounts or loans that are not yours nor have never been
- You find aliases on your credit report and have any of the above-listed problems as well

If you are not sure if you should report the potential identity theft, make your first step working with the credit reporting agency. They can often provide you with the information you need on who obtained the lines of credit.

HOW DOES IDENTITY THEFT AFFECT MY CREDIT?

Identity theft is one of the biggest problems in the financial sector and can be detrimental to victims of it. With the technological age at a peak, the ease of which thieves can access your identity is a whole new high. There are many ways to prevent identity theft and measures to take to recover after being victimized by identity thieves, but once of the best ways to guard yourself against identity theft is to understand how it works and how it affects your credit.

Credit is a fickle thing, and though it is regulated by three major reporting agencies and a mass of government bureaus, there are still mistakes made and crimes committed. It is your responsibility as a consumer to help protect your own credit and report wrongdoing. Identity theft can occur from someone stealing a wallet or purse, which usually contains an ID, checkbook with banking information, credit and other cards and sometimes a birth certificate and Social Security Card. You should never carry your SSN or birth certificate with you. There should be a copy in a home safe and the originals should be in a safety deposit box. But these items when gathered, are a prime score for a theft who can then go and use your existing cards or apply for new accounts, often before you even know the stuff is missing. Many banks and credit card companies will now help to monitor your accounts to watch for unusual spending habits and purchases, but this is not completely safe.

Once theft has done something with your identity or current accounts, it's only a matter of time before the accounts or balance default, and you start to receive harassing phone calls and letters demanding payment on a debt you know nothing about. The longer the debt has been there, the more difficult it is to get off your credit report, especially if you failed to report the identity theft or have no way to prove the account was not opened by you. This then creates bad accounts, lengthy arguing and disputes with creditors and the reporting agencies all the while your credit score is dropping, and you are finding yourself with a hard time getting the credit and approvals you have worked hard for.

This situation can be overwhelming and detrimental, and some people never recover from identity theft. It can ruin your credit, especially if you are not on guard or on top of your credit report regularly. Take the time to learn about credit reports and scores and how identity theft affects them and what you can do to find a way to prevent identity theft from happening to you. If you do become a victim of identity theft, you must report it immediately and start working to recover from the incident as soon as you notice something is wrong.

With a little work and some diligence, you can learn how identity theft affects your credit and take the steps necessary to prevent it from happening to you and your family while also putting together a recovery plan in the event of identity theft that will help you spring back fast and with minimal repercussions to your financial future and wellbeing.

HOW TO PREVENT IDENTITY THEFT FROM HAPPENING TO YOU

Identity theft is a terrible crime, and it happens to thousands of people around the country every day. With the onslaught of technology and the sophistication of the identity theft industry, you can often fall into a trap without even knowing it's right in front of you. The best way to protect yourself and your families is to follow a few easy tips that can protect you from identity theft criminals and the mind-blowing damage they can cause both emotionally and financially.

Tip #1: Protect your pieces of identity.
It's important to protect the items that share your identity. This includes your social security card, your state identification, your work identification, your car registration, and insurance cards, your birth certificate, stocks, bonds, investments, banking information, credit information, vital records and anything else that can be used to gain more information about you to use against you. If you are a mother or even a single parent, you likely carry the same information for your children. They are most vulnerable because they have not yet entered the credit world, and though their date of birth will be accessible to potential creditors, it is often not checked. You should only keep copies of your social security, vital records and all investment or banking information in your home. These should be kept in a fire-proof safe that is bolted to the

floor of a closet or secured to the house in some other way. The originals should all be in a safety deposit box with a bank you can trust.

Tip #2: Monitor your credit.
It's vitally important to purchase and monitor all three of your credit reports every year. You can order them for your children too, and it's a good idea to do so. This gives you the chance to get familiar with your credit report and learn how to look for and dispute mistakes regularly, which will allow you to catch theft in enough time to recover from the theft and work with creditors and reporting agencies to restore your credit back to the way it was.

Tip #3: Shop and spend wisely.
This is most important if you shop online. There are so many options for shopping online now, and the convenience is amazing, with the next day to your door service without ever having to go to the mall, grocery store, or another place. You can also pay bills online and

maintain your investments, but all this access leaves you wide open to thieves who can hack in and monitor the financial information you put into and save in your computer and online accounts. To help avoid this, erase your cookies regularly and only shop on sites that are certified secure.

There are many ways to prevent identity theft, and with a little practice, you and your family can help guard against identity thieves and avoid a terrible situation. Working to prevent identity theft can also make for a quicker recovery if a theft does occur and help you to bounce back with minimal damage to your credit and future borrowing power. To win the fight against identity thieves, it's important to stay diligent and always be watching for mistakes and things on your credit and accounts that just don't seem right. Train your children to do the same thing from a young age, and they will learn to respect their credit right from the start.

WHY ARE THERE MISTAKES?

Although some people may believe that mistakes on credit reports are deliberate actions by lenders, this is far from the truth, in most cases. In fact, mistakes are just that, mistakes made when someone is typing in information. Nearly all transactions that happen on credit accounts happen through automation. A computer gets your payment information from a teller who has entered it. This information is reported to the computer holding your account information. The information is then filtered one time per month to the credit bureaus, along with thousands of others' information. Perhaps one time during this process is an actual person noticing your information.

A mistake can happen from information being put into the computer system wrong, or information being missed. It could be that the credit card company's machines read your "9" as a "0," and therefore, you were not marked as making payment in full for the month. Many potential mistakes can happen.

LOCATE THE CREDIT REPORT MISTAKES

There are going to be mistaken in your credit report. The number of mistakes is not as important as noticing them. Each of the three credit bureaus legally must take into consideration the information that you provide to them about mistakes. They do not have to make the changes you request unless the credit lender that put the information there is unable to prove that the information is correct.

In the next chapter, we'll outline how to get those mistakes off the report. Before that, though, you need to know what types of mistakes to look for and why you need to remove them. Don't skip this step. If you fail to remove all the information that is incorrect on your credit report, you may not be getting it as clean as you could be.

TYPES OF CREDIT MISTAKES TO FIND

While mistakes do happen, that does not mean that they are irreversible. The following are some of the most common mistakes you will find on your credit report that should be reported to the credit bureau. You should report these to have them removed.

Remember, it only takes a few minutes to scan your credit report, but looking at the details is where you will find most mistakes. Take the time to go through your credit report with your spouse, if you have one, to ensure that the information being report is accurate, even with their usage of credit that is potentially in your own name.

INCORRECT ACCOUNT INFORMATION

One of the largest problems that individuals have with their credit report is information on it that is simply not accurate or does not seem to be their own. Depending on how long you have had credit, you may not remember all the credit lines you have. For example, you may have signed up for a store credit card ten years ago and never used it. As mentioned earlier, older accounts that have no bad information on them (such as late payments, collection activity) should not be removed from your account. This is especially true of open but not used credit accounts. These establish the length of time you have had credit, which is a good thing for most credit scores.

Look at the accounts closely. Is the following information correct?

- Is the account one that you have opened? If not, and it has a balance, report it to the credit agency. Follow up with the company about the account.

- Is the account listed providing the right balance information? The account may be on a list up to two months behind the current balance since lenders report only one time per month on the account.

- Is the information on the credit limit, credit type, lender, and account holder correct? Your monthly payment may not be accurate, which could stop some lenders from lending to you down the road.

- Is the payment history accurate? Without including the last two months, is the past payment history, right? Are the payments listed as late that are not? This should be in the report, if so.

- Is there any other information being reported that is inaccurate? This could be collection activity, judgments, information about bankruptcies that is incorrect, or other information. These should be in the report.

Missing information is also possible. In most cases, this is not a problem, as no information does not necessarily hurt your credit history. Still, there will be times when you want the most accurate representation. If the account has the wrong opening date, consider reporting this.

Go through each of your credit accounts to find out what is incorrect on them. Report problems through the steps outlined in the next chapter.

OLD NOTATIONS ON ACCOUNTS

Another potential problem you may notice on your credit report is old information. There is a lot of information available about old debts, accounts, and inquiries that are on your credit report. What should be there, and when should it just fade into the past?

While many people would say that you should pay all your debts, it is important to note the legalities of paying the debt. If you have a debt that goes unpaid for seven years, and the lender has not made any communication with you over those seven years, you legally are no longer responsible for the debt. In addition to this, debts can remain on your credit report for up to seven years. After that point, it should fall off your report forgotten, unless the debt is active, such as a credit card account you are still using.

What is important to know about this is that if there is a debt being reported on your credit report where there has been no activity for a full seven years, it should be removed from the report, especially if it is unpaid debt. If you have a credit card that has a good record of accomplishment, but you have paid it off and no longer use it, this can again serve as a good history for your credit usage and should be in place.

Old marks on your credit report should automatically be removed, but this does not always happen. In the cases where it does not, it is up to you to have it taken off. Here are some notes to keep in mind:

- Old debt unpaid where there is no communication with you should have removal after two years.
- Old credit accounts should disappear after two years, though some with good credit history may remain longer (and that is good!)
- Bankruptcies and judgments passed against you will remain on your credit report for up to ten years. These cannot have removal until after that time.

You have the right to dispute claims that you find that are older than allowed to be. This can be an important tool for improving your credit report, especially if the older accounts have negative marks on them.

MONITOR AND LIMIT INQUIRIES

As mentioned earlier, inquiries on your credit report will detract from it. It is inevitable to have some, especially if you are looking for new lines of credit. The key is to keep them as low as possible. On your credit report, there is a separation between the two types of inquiries, those that affect your credit score and those that do not. The goal is to monitor both, though. If you are prone to accepting credit cards if offers are sent to you, sign up for a do not mail registry. You can opt-out of future credit card offers by visiting the website of the Consumer Credit Reporting Industry at OptOutPrescreen.com. You can also locate the Federal Trade Commission for your state and request that these offers stop that way, too.

While you are watching your credit report, keep an eye on the credit inquiries, too. You must ensure that those that count against you are monitored. Report anything that should not be there. Also, if they do not come off your report within two years, these, too, should come to the credit reporting industry.

What about the way that you use those credit inquiries? The best way to keep them off your credit report is to ensure that you are not over applying for lines of credit. Here are some tips:

- Choose one or two cards to apply for at any time. Limit the number of applications you file within 3 to 6-month periods.

- When you are shopping for the best insurance or credit card, ask for quotes from the service providers without allowing them to pull a credit report. Let them know the approximate credit score you have. This will allow you to compare several lines of credit or insurance companies without having to subject your credit report to too many inquiries.

- For larger loans, such as a home mortgage loan or car loan, again obtain quotes for loans based on your approximate credit score. This also protects your credit. Many lenders allow you to do this right online. If they do not, look elsewhere for the loan you need.

INQUIRIES

As mentioned earlier, there is a need to monitor the number of inquiries you have on your credit report. Inquiries are placed on your report whenever someone has requested a copy of your credit report. For example, if you apply for a credit card, the lender will request a company of your credit score and report from the credit bureau to find out how much of a risk you are. When they do this, after receiving information from you requesting this account, the inquiry is on the credit report.

Too many inquiries can downgrade your credit report. For this reason, be selected to apply for any credit or allowing any company to pull a credit report on you. This includes insurance companies and businesses that want you to work for them.

If you spot inquiries you have not approved, you can have them removed from your credit report. It is essential to be sure you have not approved this inquiry, though. To do so, you will need to use the information provided to your advantage. The inquiry will include the name of the company who pulled the report and their contact information. Call them directly and request information about why they have requested a copy of your credit report. They will tell you.

Many times, you will not recognize the actual lender's name on the credit report, but you will be able to remember the transaction after you have called them and asked a question. If, after speaking with the company, you still do not have any memory of this information, the best course of action is to report the inquiry to the credit bureau. They will then force the company to show proof that you requested the inquiry and remove it if it is not possible to verify the information.

Credit inquiries will stay on your credit report for up to two years. Be sure to keep an eye on them over time and to report any mistakes you may have.

IDENTITY MISTAKES

While we mentioned identity theft, there may be other identity problems on your credit report that are not nearly as serious. Here, someone has not actually stolen your identity, but rather the spelled your name wrong, given you someone else's address or otherwise made mistakes with your credit reporting.

Many times, these errors do not matter. If there is a missing letter in your name, likely, the mistake has not affected your credit score in any way. Still, you may wish to clean up your credit report and remove this information from it.

In the following chapter, we talk about reporting processes for removing credit-related information. The same process is not followed for identity mistakes such as your name, your employer information, your address, or other identifiable information. Instead, you will need to call the credit bureau directly to report these problems. Some of this information is unable to be removed from your credit report, and the agency will let you know that. Other mistakes can receive attention right away.

It may be important for you to update your employer's information. This is done over the phone once there is proof of your identity. You may also want to update your address if it is not correct. You may not be able to remove an address you once lived at, though. If you have never lived at the address, report this to the agency.

HOW TO RESTORE YOUR CREDIT AFTER IDENTITY THEFT

Identity theft can be a terrible thing, and when left unnoticed or unreported can ruin your credit and borrowing power for the long term. Though identity theft can cause major problems with your credit and drop your credit score dramatically, there are ways to work to recover from identity theft and restore your credit to what it once was. One of the first things to remember is the quicker identity theft is reported, the easier it is to remove from your credit. Regardless of whether you reported quickly or were too embarrassed to come forward, you need to contact your credit accounts, the agencies that house your personal information and the police to make a complaint and start the process to recovery.

The first step is to try and find out the extent of the damage caused, and you can start with that by ordering and printing your current credit reports from all three agencies. You then need to sit down and go over them with a fine-toothed comb and highlight anything that you don't remember, is completely incorrect, or you are unsure of. Then take the time to contact the creditors listed for those accounts in question and get as much information about the accounts or incorrect purchases made on the account. They should send you hard copies in the mail, and this will become part of the dispute and evidence folder you are going to build. Do this with all affected accounts, creditors and agencies, gathering as much information as possible with each one. Once you have done that, make two or three copies of all the evidence you have. You will want to file a copy of everything with your police report, plus keep your own copies when it comes time to turn everything in for dispute.

Many companies now allow you to call and report a theft on the account and will freeze the transactions while you and they investigate the situation. This can stop the debt from incurring in the first place and falling into a default status while you are trying to take care of the situation. Take advantage of this feature on any affected accounts that have them.

At the end of each of your credit reports are the instructions for how to file a dispute through that credit reporting agency. Make sure you read it over a couple of times and understand it completely. This can be the difference between a successful dispute and one that gets tossed in the trash. You must follow the guidelines completely and understand there is a waiting period where the creditors get to investigate and respond to the items you are disputing.

Regardless of the level of identity theft that has occurred, there are ways to bounce back and preserve your credit for future borrowing and good credit standing. Your credit score will take longer to bounce back than the information on the credit report. This is because it is not updated as often. Always keep track of all your accounts and what their current status is. Also, keep all important papers in a fire-proof safe and the originals in a safe-deposit box with a bank you can trust. With a little diligence and some hard work, you can bounce back from identity theft and protect yourself against being a victim in the future while still maintaining a good credit rating and fulfilling your financial dreams.

TAKE IT STEP BY STEP

Your credit report is the only piece of information that most lenders receive about you when you apply for a loan through them. It is essential to consider what is on your report and what should not be there. Go through the credit report one line at a time. It is often helpful to print it out and use the paper version to track what you have reported.

The first time you pull your credit report, you are sure to find more than a few mistakes. It may take you some time to locate them all and to get them repaired. Over time, fewer will be reported as you are more conscious of who you are giving your credit information to.

It is essential to go through your report at the very least one time per year to locate any potential problems with it. You should report problems as they happen!

IT TAKES TIME

One of the hardest elements to come from the entire process of improving your credit report is that it takes time. Sometimes, it takes a long time.

Those who find errors in their credit report will have the ability to remove them, which may or may not give you a boost in your credit score. This depends greatly on the type of mistake you have removed.

For example, if you remove problems with:

- Your name
- Your address
- Past employers
- Other personal information

Chances are good that you will not see any change in your credit score since these items do not have a direct link to it.

On the other hand, if you find mistakes and have them removed like those in the following list:

- Debts that are not your own that are removed
- Outdated debts that are negatively impacting your credit score
- Collection accounts or judgments removed
- Inquiries
- Late payments, missing payments
- Over the limit reports

Or similar types of items, you should see a rise in your credit report for doing so. The amount of increase is unknown since these complex formulas are not made public knowledge. The key is that over the long term, such as in the next six months to a year, you will no longer fell effects by the negative mistakes, and this will help to boost the ongoing credit score you have.

TIPS FOR INCREASING YOUR CREDIT SCORE QUICKLY

There is no one way to raise your credit score. It is a combined effort of everything you do throughout your life, having to do with credit. The key here is to make the best choices overall. It is difficult and time-consuming at best, but ultimately it will give you the best results overall. Maintaining your credit report and credit score is perhaps the longest journey you will be on throughout your life. There is never a time when you can take a break.

Some things to do to ensure the highest credit score is in reach:

1. Get your credit report clean of any errors on it by reporting and disputing these with each of the three credit reporting agencies, TransUnion, Equifax, and Experian.

2. Keep an eye on your credit report. At least one time a year, pull each report, examine it for potential mistakes, and keep it clean.

3. Don't make payments late. One of the worst things you can do is send in your payment late. This is an instant warning sign to potential lenders: he or she is struggling with debt; beware! Send your payment in at least a week before the due date to ensure punctuality.

4. Do not go over your credit limit, like late payments; this is another instance of struggling to make payments.

5. Keep your debts low. Pay off as much of or all your debt each month. This shows to lenders you are a good credit risk and that you deserve more credit available to you.

6. Stay on top of the changes credit bureaus and Congress make to credit reporting. Small changes can make a significant

difference in the way credit reporting happens and, therefore, what your credit is.

7. Use credit when you need to but keep yourself in check.

8. Don't request multiple lines of credit at one time. When shopping for the best rates on a credit card, insurance product, or home loan, do so using estimated credit scores rather than allowing several companies to pull your report.

9. Keep your personal information personal. This includes your Social Security Number, address, and historical information about you. Report any risks of identity theft as soon as you see them.

10.   Live within your CASH means. In other words, make sure that 90 percent or more of your purchases are made using cash. Get off the credit lifestyle, and you may find

that your credit score goes up and you have more money in your pocket each month.

It does take a long time to build a successful credit report, but the process itself is one that teaches you how to use money wisely. It does not matter what has brought you to this point today. The only thing that truly makes a difference is what happens tomorrow.

Clean up your credit report first. Then, and ongoing, maintain it and use credit wisely. You will then have more doors open to you each month, and you will have credit available to you when you need it.

Choosing and Creating Good Accounts to Boost Your Credit

Credit can be a fickle thing and complicated to those who are unsure of how credit works. Credit is a billion-dollar a year industry, and while most of that represents a debt that families and individuals are struggling to get out from under, it also represents the possibilities that credit can offer. When handled appropriately and with smart decision making, credit can be a great thing that offers opportunities and advancement to you. Most people think of credit as to how you can get a house, a vehicle, or other loans for items of value, but credit is also used to judge character about a person when they are applying for a rental, a job or other life advancement.

Take the time to choose and create the right accounts to reflect good credit and then maintain those accounts to boost your credit rating and score for the ultimate level of possibility in the future. So, how do you know which are good accounts to have and which are ones to avoid? Many different types of accounts can be obtained, and many of them are offered with enticingly low-interest rates or high limits. The first step in determining accounts that are worth your time is to read the fine print and see whether the low-interest rate will balloon after a couple of months or whether the high limit will create a level of temptation you may not be able to avoid. Also, only work with banks or other companies you know and trust, try to avoid ones that are new, unstable, or unknown. Besides being a smart choice for investing your time and money in, larger, more well-known lending companies are better to have on your credit report because they lend more weight when others are considering lending to you.

Good accounts should be smaller ones. You can pay off in full before the due date and should be for things you need or reflect a starter account status. Starter accounts are those that are small or through trustworthy companies with slightly lower standards than other companies. They are often jewelry store accounts, store credit accounts, cell phone company agreements, and other small accounts. These accounts are perfect for first-time borrowers or for those recovering from bankruptcy that essentially must start over with their credit building. Once you have been given a chance with a small account, it's up to you to be responsible with it and pay your payments on time and in full each month to keep them in good standing and avoid going into debt or financial hardship.

The longer a good account is in good standing on your credit, the higher it can push your credit rating and score. Large lenders, like real estate and car loans, like to see that you have a few good, solid accounts that you have had for years and never been late or defaulted on. This shows that you can not only make smart financial decisions but that you can also maintain loans and budgeting over an extended period, which will help them feel they are making a smart choice by investing in you.

Regardless of the starter or small accounts, you decide to go with, take the time to do some research and learn about how small and starter accounts can help you define your credit status and create good credit over time and through commitment. It's important to take the time to invest in your own future by learning about the financial world and how loans and credit work. They may seem intimidating and like something you cannot understand, but with a little work and possibly a little help, you can learn the tools and habits you need for a successful financial future. Aren't you and your family's future worth it?

Your credit report is one of the most important tools you have in the financial world. It defines who you are to lenders of all types. Removing errors from your credit report, or "cleaning it up" is only one part of the process. You need to ensure that you are doing everything possible to keep your credit report in stellar shape so that you also look great in the eyes of a credit card company or home mortgage lender.

Part of this process is to tackle the errors on your credit report. That is the right place to start since this information is hurting you for no real reason. As you wait to find out if the errors will be removed by the credit reporting agency, take some time to work through the following steps. These ten methods for improving your credit score are simple and straightforward, but they also provide you with the resources you need. They may not be easy to do, and most of them require time. Nevertheless, making key decisions right now will help you to get back on track and have a high-ranking credit score.

Keep in mind the importance of a quality credit score. With many banks and lenders tightening their lending practices, they simply are not giving out the types of loans you may be used to getting with an average or lower credit score. In fact, if your score is not in the upper 700's, you may be unable to get a home loan without a significant amount down. The days of having a 400-credit score and getting a great line of credit may not be back anytime soon. Therefore, take steps right now to improve your credit score so you do not have to hope that you can get that home of your dreams.

CONTACTING THE CREDIT BUREAUS

In most situations, you will want to work through the credit bureaus directly to have any errors or mistakes removed from your credit report. You can do this easily right on the company's website.

All credit reporting agencies have the process of removing credit mistakes online now. It used to be that you needed to call or mail a letter to the credit bureau to get the process going. Now, credit bureaus have made the process quite simple to do. You simply need to sign in to the account you had credited when you obtained the copy of your credit report, fill in some basic information, and send it off to the lender. Of course, it is a bit more complex than this, but the process is not nearly as complicated as you may expect it to be.

MAKING THE MOST OUT OF CLAIMS

Filing a claim against something that has been reported on your credit report may feel overwhelming, but the process is very straight forward and only takes a few minutes to get started. It is not the job of the credit reporting agency to verify the claim further than relying on the information that is provided to them. In other words, don't be angry with or treat the credit bureau wrongly as most likely, the item was reported incorrectly to them.
Nevertheless, they are working with you to ensure your credit report is the most up to date and accurate as it can be.

Do take the time to be thorough with your claims, and be sure to follow up on them. Provide information to the credit bureau about why you feel that the information is incorrect. "This information is not right." If you type this into the report, chances are good that they will need a bit more information. You may be required to checkboxes to explain the situation further.

"This account was closed on May 5th, 2003, after being fully paid off by a check I have the receipt for." This is much more thorough and gives enough information for the creditor to go back and track down the problem. You may be 100 percent right in both cases, but if not, enough information is available, it can be difficult to prove.

Be patient, too. The credit bureaus are not very friendly in terms of providing you with details about the process and where it stands. Therefore, there is no benefit in calling the company repeatedly and requesting more information.

Also, be sure to check your other credit reports for the same or similar mistakes. It is a good sign if the error only appears on one report even though the other two credit bureaus also report on that account. Yet, the same mistake may have been reported to all three. Go through the accounts and follow up!

Finding mistakes on your credit report is vital to improving your credit score and the way that lenders see you. If you do not take the time to do this, you may find your credit report is suffering. Avoid mistakes. Make sure your credit report is accurate by following this process at least one time each year.

YOU'VE FOUND THE PROBLEM: NOW WHAT?

You know the information being reported about you is incorrect. You are probably a bit angry and annoyed that lenders see this information, and there is no simple way to remove the information. If anything, the fact that it will take up to two months to have it removed can also be annoying. Still, the process is in place to ensure that the most accurate information is on your credit report.

Once you have found an error, you will need to fill out a form stating so at the credit bureau's website. This part is easy. You likely will need to provide the following information:

- The item you are disputing (your credit card, your mortgage loan, etc.)
- The reason for your dispute (it wasn't late, the information is inaccurate or incomplete, etc.)

- Any additional information on why this is the case (proof of a canceled check or statements to back up your claim.)

Generally, the information regarding your proof is not collected from you. Rather, the credit bureau will require that the credit card company or lender verify this information. They will need to show proof that the claim they have made to the credit reporting agency is, in fact, true. In other words, the burden of proof is on the lender, not on you, the borrower.

This is a good thing because it is often more difficult to prove something is true than to have to prove that something is not true. Once you file a claim with the credit-reporting agency, the creditor must show proof that your claim was accurate.

Here is a closer look at the process:

1. You pull a copy of your credit report. You find an error on your report.

2. You contact the credit bureau and let them know this is not accurate. For example, it may be an account that is no longer one you have and does not carry a balance though the report says it is.

3. The credit reporting agency will then contact the creditor. They let them know of your dispute with their claim.

4. The creditor must dig through their records and find the information. Generally, this is available on computers and is accurate. There could have been a mistake when the information was reported. Or, there may be inaccurate information in their system. In either case, they need to show that the information is accurate.

5. The credit lender has 30 days from the time you have filed the complaint to straighten

out the situation. Most lenders want to report accurately.

Then what, you may ask. Once the claim is with the creditor, the credit reporting bureau must wait to hear back from the lender. Is this information accurate? If so, can they prove it?

If they find that the information is accurate and they have proof that it is, the lender's claim is reported to the credit reporting agency, who then leaves the information on your credit report. There can be no further disputes against the information after that decision. If you have overwhelming proof of the situation, contact the credit bureau again requesting help to resolving the problem. Generally, though, a paper trail is the only way to disprove their claim.

If the creditor comes back and says that they cannot prove the claim they have filed against you, for whatever reason, the credit reporting agency will then remove it from your report. This may help to boost your credit score right away, or it may have no effect, depending on the type of report, the length of time since it was reported, and other factors. The key here is that it has removal, and you no longer must live with the mistake.

If the creditor misses the 30-day deadline for coming back to you about the claim, then the credit reporting agency will remove the mark from your credit report as it cannot be proven. As with the opposite scenario, once this decision occurs, it cannot have a reversal.

In any case, within that 30 periods, you will not know what is happening. But, after the report has been decided on, you will. The credit reporting agency will report the information to you in a letter, mailed directly to your home. This information is usually the final answer to the problem, yet it is nearly always the most accurate result, too.

GO TO THE RIGHT CREDIT BUREAU

The first step is to go back to the credit bureau's website. You will need to report the error to the individual credit bureau that s reporting the problem. For example, if you find a mistake on your Experian account, you will need to go to Experian to have it removed. At the same time, though, realize that if the mistake has been reported on all three credit reports, you may need to file a claim against each one. This will allow you to get it removed from each of the company's reports.

Most credit bureaus require you to create an account and password when you sign in to view your credit report. This is helpful because it allows you to come back to your report whenever you need to (they are generally available to you for 30 days from the time you have requested them.) Head back to the website and log in.

Once there, you will find a link on the home page, usually, that allows you to "dispute" the report or item. This is generally a link that is located on this page, which will take you to a much more in-depth form to fill out. You will be fine with the process if you have a printed copy of your credit report on hand to allow you to navigate easily where you need to go.

Sometimes, the companies will allow you to click a link located directly next to the report that's been filed. For example, next to your credit card lender's name and account information, there may be a link to dispute a claim. There will be another link on the next lender's information for the same reason. This is perhaps one of the easiest ways to report an error on your credit report.
Now that you are there, what should you do?

HOW TO CLEAN IT UP

Now that you have taken the time to find the mistakes on your credit report, the next step is to get them off there!

The credit bureaus are only collecting information. They never see accounts or payments. They do not work between you and the lender, either. The first course of action for you to take if you notice a problem is to go to that lender and ask questions. This is particularly helpful for recent information or transactions. For example, perhaps you had noticed that payment did not post or that someone had a listing as late when it was on time.

Your creditor does have the ability to change remarks left on your credit report. They do not always do this instantly, though. It may take until the next reporting that they provide to the credit bureaus. What is important is that you call them and let them know of the mistake. They can then give you instant access to information. Do they have your payment listed as being late? Did they make a mistake in your credit usage? This information should be understood by you before filing a claim directly with the credit reporting agencies. That way, you know what the facts are and can deal with them appropriately.

Calling your creditor and asking them questions about your credit report is an option to consider. They may or may not be able to clear up the problem, though. You will still need to ensure that the mistakes are removed from your actual credit report, too. Even if they assure you that the mistakes will receive removal in the next 30 to 60 days, follow up and make sure that this happens.

THE BASICS OF CREDIT CLEAN UP

Credit can be a fickle thing, and if you don't know much about credit, your credit report, or score and how credit works, it can seem overwhelming to try and find ways to fix or clean it up. As overwhelming as credit practices may seem, there are ways to clean up your credit and plan for a better financial future with smarter spending and borrowing practices.

There are four main ways to clean up your credit, and the more cohesively you use them together, the better the result at the end. This chapter will briefly go through the four areas and how to take part in them. Through your research, you are likely to come across more in-depth information that will play a part in working with the information provided here to give you the best results in cleaning up your credit.

The first way to start your journey toward better credit and a higher credit score if to work on a payoff or debt management plan. The more you ignore your debt, the worse it gets, and the harder to fix. You need to first get all three of your current credit reports and lay them out in front of you. Take the time to use a highlighter and highlight all the accounts that are currently open and have a balance. Some of these are likely past due, while others may not be. To get a complete look at what you need to pay off, you need to highlight them all. This should NOT include monthly living expenses like utilities, rent, or other accounts that may be listed on your credit report. This is only the debt you need to get out from under. The next step to forming a debt pay off plan to consider the highest balances or highest interest rates first since these are more harmful to your credit, though the smaller accounts may be easier to pay off. Remember, while you are paying off larger debts with larger payments, you must still maintain the minimum payments on monthly accounts and living expenses to keep from worsening your debt.

The next step in the credit cleanup process should be to consider the good accounts you have and work hard to keep them in positive standing. These accounts will help to steady and improve your credit when you get the bad accounts paid off. When you have paid off the bad and past-due accounts, you can consider adding a good or small account to keep in good standing but don't consider adding anything until you have dug yourself out of the hole you are currently in.

Next, you want to check over your credit report for errors. This can happen by accident or through the presence of identity theft. Either way, you need to find it and dispute it. Each credit reporting agency has its own dispute policies and procedures, and you will need to read through and follow them accordingly to dispute incorrect items on your credit report. Often this information will print at the end of your credit report and should be readily available on the agency web sites as well.

The last and probably most important thing to consider when working to clean up your credit is to form and set up a plan for future financial success. You need to be able to handle money smartly and avoid getting back into the same situation or having to work so hard again. To do this, you need to learn to live within your means and learn the difference between need and want. This can be especially hard if you've become accustomed to a certain standard of living or have friends with a higher standard of living than you can afford. You need to be honest with yourself and with others about the life you can currently have, this will help you be about to reach the life you want in the future.

CREDIT CLEAN UP: DISPUTE INCORRECT INFORMATION FROM YOUR CREDIT REPORT

When you are working to clean up your credit, the job can seem overwhelming and too much to handle. To make it easier, there are a few simple ways to go about the process that, when used together, form the best results and more peaceful you. One of the steps to the process of credit cleanup is to inspect each of your credit reports and dispute any incorrect information you find. This is vital to not only maintaining good credit but is also important when cleaning up your bad credit and preventing and catching identity theft. Ideally, you should purchase your credit reports once a year and go over them with a fine-tooth comb and dispute anything you find to be incorrect.

There are three major credit reporting agencies Experian, Equifax, and TransUnion. They all have a web site with ordering instructions on how to pay for and download or print your credit report. Some sites offer all three of the reports at once and other services as well. Be careful when considering these sites as they can be a little shady and want you to join as a member to receive their services or special prices. It's best to stick with ordering and printing your reports straight from the source.

Once you have your credit reports take a few minutes to print each one and staple them together to keep them from getting mixed up. While you will be going through them separately, you will want to compare the information between them as well to check for discrepancies. Once you have everything in order, find a comfortable place, you can concentrate on a highlighter and a pen to mark things of question you find.

Generally, the credit report is separated into different categories starting with your personal information, residential information, and employment information. Though the focus of a credit report is one of the accounts, you need to look through these areas to check for the name, address, and employment errors because these could be a sign of identity theft. Next, move on to the accounts, collections, judgments, and other sections you need to look for accounts that you have paid that are not marked as paid. Incorrect balances, accounts and other information. Not only do you need to mark the items you feel are incorrect, but then you will need to go through your financial records to find receipts and other levels of proof to show the information is incorrect. This is your burden to prove the information on the reports is not correct and you may need to contact the companies the accounts are through to try and find out their side of it too, to get the information changed to reflect the right information.

At the end of all credit reports are the dispute information and procedures that each credit reporting agency uses. Make sure to follow them down to the exact letter to keep your claim from getting thrown out. The creditors have a time frame to look over the dispute and have up to ninety days to make the change, and then the credit reporting agency can make the change or act for you. It does take some time to get the wrong information corrected, but the time is well worth it, and you could be saving your self-money and interest rates in the future.

CREDIT CLEAN UP: PAYING OFF DEBT

Cleaning up your credit can seem a little daunting and overwhelming when you are first looking for a way out from under your debt. Before embarking on your journey of debt recovery, there are some things you need to know to make the process easier and more successful. One of the keyways of cleaning up your credit is by paying off your debt. Debt pays off-plan is the best way to start working toward a future without debt. There are a few steps toward forming a debt pay off a plan that can make the process a good one. Those steps are as follows and should be considered when putting together your pay off plan.

Step 1: The first things you need to do are get a grasp on your level of debt and face it head-on. You need to order and print them out. They can be ordered on the Equifax and other credit reporting agency web sites, and then you can print them out. The reason printing them is the best way to handle it is because you can then spread everything out in front of you and get a good look at the items on there. Also, pull all your recent statements and bills and put them on the table or work surface with your credit reports. If you are more about computers, then use Excel to create the following list, and they formulate a cell for a grand total at the bottom or top of the list. The list should include the creditor, creditor contact information, due date, monthly payment, interest rate and current balance. Cross-check the information you pull from your bill pile with that from your credit reports to make sure there are no doubles and that the information is the most up to date as possible.

Step 2: Next, you need to highlight or star the accounts with the highest balances (top five) and the highest interest rates. These are your most detrimental accounts. These are the accounts you want to focus your extra money and attention on. Keep in mind though that you still need to pay the minimums on your other accounts while you are concentrating on the larger accounts one at a time. This will keep you from defaulting further and getting more into trouble.

Step 3: You should always attempt to negotiate and pay off companies if you have the resources to do so. If you have access to a lump sum or have close to the balance of any of the accounts, then you need to get on the phone and negotiate down the debt with them and offer them a settlement. This can get rid of debt quickly while still saving you money. If some of your creditors are unwilling to budge on balance, then ask for a lower interest rate.

These are all ways to help you find the best way to pay off your debt, and when used together can have the best success in forming a debt pay off the plan that you can stick with and will find success with. Paying off debt is a big task, and it will take tenacity and strive to see it through to the end, but when you get there, the push and drive will be replaced by pride and relief and, hopefully, a renewed sense of respect for credit and the money you make.

CREDIT CLEAN UP: MAKE A PLAN FOR THE FUTURE

Credit clean up can be a daunting task, especially when you have no idea which direction to go. Once you have taken on the task of paying off debt, adding good accounts, and disputing the incorrect information on your credit report, the time has come to set a plan into action for the future to avoid getting yourself into the same financial mess. A plan can be a simple as giving yourself some ground rules around spending and money management, or as intense as hiring a money manager or freezing your credit cards. You need to think about the methods it will take to get you into a habit and practice of spending smart and efficiently.

Money should be respected, after all, you work hard for it, and you should be able to enjoy life with it, within reason. Many people find themselves living above their means and often have such a hard time reeling back in after a financial crisis, but planning for the future does not have to mean depriving yourself of all the things you love or time out with your friends, in fact, it shouldn't. Like with dieting, if you deprive yourself, you are more prone to failure than if you just learn a healthier approach.

While you were working through your debt pay off plan and other aspects of debt management, there should have been a period when you kept track of your daily spending to see where your money was going and how you could conserve and pull from that to pay off the debt. You should pull this list out now and look at it in a different light. Before you were living from the list, taking everything for granted and during your pay off time, you were living without any extras, and incomplete deprivation now is the time to find balance. Through the time of depravity, you should have to build a more solid sense of what is important and what is not. Do you really need to spend $7 a day on an iced mocha when you are trying to lose weight? No way, you are sabotaging yourself and wasting money. Even if you don't drink coffee, you understand the point. Go back through the list and star the things that were unnecessary and that you have learned to live without and highlight the little things you missed. If the items you missed are still hard on your monthly budget, then look for ways to cut them down a bit. If you can't live without a salon visit for hair and nails, instead of going once a week, go once every two weeks instead. Stylists and nail technicians all know ways to make your cut and manicure last longer. Take advantage of this and save a little money.

Now that you know what areas you can survive without and how to make your money stretch so that you are living within your means, you can relax a little and continue your journey toward a brighter financial future. With a few little changes and some self-discipline, you can find a way to start new healthy spending habits and get rid of the old. This will round out your credit cleanup work and help you to avoid falling into the same situation in the future.

Plus, wouldn't it be great to save for that dream vacation?

CHOOSING AND CREATING GOOD ACCOUNTS TO BOOST YOUR CREDIT

Credit can be a fickle thing and complicated to those who are unsure of how credit works. Credit is a billion-dollar a year industry, and while most of that represents a debt that families and individuals are struggling to get out from under, it also represents the possibilities that credit can offer. When handled appropriately and with smart decision making, credit can be a great thing that offers opportunities and advancement to you. Most people think of credit as to how you can get a house, a vehicle, or other loans for items of value, but credit is also used to judge character about a person when they are applying for a rental, a job or other life advancement.

Take the time to choose and create the right accounts to reflect good credit and then maintain those accounts to boost your credit rating and score for the ultimate level of possibility in the future. So, how do you know which are good accounts to have and which are ones to avoid?

Many different types of accounts can be obtained, and many of them are offered with enticingly low-interest rates or high limits. The first step in determining accounts that are worth your time is to read the fine print and see whether the low-interest rate will balloon after a couple of months or whether the high limit will create a level of temptation you may not be able to avoid. Also, only work with banks or other companies you know and trust, try to avoid ones that are new, unstable, or unknown. Besides being a smart choice for investing your time and money in, larger, more well-known lending companies are better to have on your credit report because they lend more weight when others are considering lending to you.

Good accounts should be smaller ones. You can pay off in full before the due date and should be for things you need or reflect a starter account status. Starter accounts are those that are small or through trustworthy companies with slightly lower standards than other companies. They are often jewelry store accounts, store credit accounts, cell phone company agreements, and other small accounts. These accounts are perfect for first-time borrowers or for those recovering from bankruptcy that essentially must start over with their credit building. Once you have been given a chance with a small account, it's up to you to be responsible with it and pay your payments on time and in full each month to keep them in good standing and avoid going into debt or financial hardship.

The longer a good account is in good standing on your credit, the higher it can push your credit rating and score. Large lenders, like real estate and car loans, like to see that you have a few good, solid accounts that you have had for years and never been late or defaulted on. This shows that you can not only make smart financial decisions but that you can also maintain loans and budgeting over an extended period, which will help them feel they are making a smart choice by investing in you.

Regardless of the starter or small accounts, you decide to go with, take the time to do some research and learn about how small and starter accounts can help you define your credit status and create good credit over time and through commitment. It's important to take the time to invest in your own future by learning about the financial world and how loans and credit work. They may seem intimidating and like something you cannot understand, but with a little work and possibly a little help, you can learn the tools and habits you need for a successful financial future. Aren't you and your family's future worth it?

SAMPLE LETTERS:

Here are examples of dispute letters that have proven to be effective...

DISPUTE LETTERS

There are three ways to communicate with credit offices about your disputes; online, by telephone, or by mail. They strongly recommend that letters are sent as letters do not suffer from' techno' glitches and black holes, even though electronically, it might be quicker and quicker than before. Writing a letter is working. It provides a hard copy, and the paper trail provides evidence of the dispute.

To file a dispute in writing, you must send a certified letter to the creditor with the required return receipt. You may send certified letters to your local post office. You may keep copies of your dispute letters and any enclosures.

Your credit report will provide up-to-date contact information and instructions for telephone and written disputes

When writing your letters, you need to make them brief and to the point. You do not need to write excuses; they'll be ignored by the credit bureau. In each letter include...

- ☐ Your full name as it appears on your credit report
- ☐ Your current address, phone number, email address, and social security number
- ☐ A statement instructing the company to investigate the disputed item
- ☐ The item in question, along with the account number
- ☐ A reason why you believe the information is incorrect or invalid. Be concise.
- ☐ Copies of any supporting documents, as well as a copy of your credit report.

Your letters will include the account

information which you are disputing. It is best to just clip and paste the entire entry from the credit report to your letter. It's faster, easy, and much more accurate as opposed to re-typing the detail.

The reason *why* you are disputing each item is very important. On those items which are in error, simply state the error; *'wrong dates,' 'a closed, not open account,' 'over 7 years old', 'incorrect balances listed,' 'incorrect past-due information,' 'not my account,' 'do not recognize the account,' 'incorrect type of credit,' 'actions stated never happened,' 'erroneous payment entries'* and so on.

When disputing negative information, the most common reasons the account is being disputed include; "*do not recognize this account,*" "*invalid account information,*" 'a closed, not open account,' "has been paid in full,' 'has always been paid promptly,' 'the account is over 7 years old', 'not my account,' "has never

114

been delinquent,' "incorrect type of credit,' 'actions stated never happened,' 'erroneous payment entries,' 'not my account,' 'I never agreed to the terms' and so on.

Don't forget you must send your letter by certified mail. The addresses set up to receive disputes should appear on your credit report, or you may use the ones below...

Credit Report Disputes
Equifax Information Services LLC
P.O. Box 740256 Atlanta, GA 30374
1-866-640-2273
http://www.equifax.com

Credit Report Disputes TransUnion
Consumer Solutions
P.O. Box 6790 Fullerton, CA 92834
1-800-916-8800
http://www.transunion.com

Credit Report Disputes Experian
National Consumer Assistance Center
P.O. Box 9530 Allen, TX 75013
1-888-397-3742
http://www.experian.com

The following section will show you examples of effective dispute letters you can use.

ADDING POSITIVE ACCOUNTS

January 15, 2019

Attn: Credit Report Disputes Experian
National Consumer Assistance Center
P.O. Box 2002 Allen, TX 75013

Dear Sir or Madam,

This letter is a formal request to add missing information to my credit report. The following account(s) do not currently appear on my credit report and should be included in my credit report immediately.

You will note that this account is in good standing and can be verified with the information I have supplied in this letter.

Per the federal Fair Credit Reporting Act (FCRA), I respectfully request you investigate my claim and, if after your investigation, you find my claim to be valid and accurate, I request that you immediately update my credit report. This account is:

Ashley Furniture #202-400-01
123 Main Street
Columbus, Ohio 78522
147-332-3232
Date opened: January 2016 Amount: $432
Terms: 42 months

I thank you for your consideration and cooperation. If you have any questions concerning this matter, I can be reached at the contact information listed below.

Sincerely,

Your First and Last Name
Your Mailing Address
City, State Zip
Your Telephone Number
youremail@gmail.com

SSN: 000-00-0000

Enclosures: (List what you are enclosing.)

DISPUTING INACCURATE INFORMATION AND/OR ERRORS

March 25, 2017

Attn: Credit Report Disputes Experian
National Consumer Assistance Center
P.O. Box 2002 Allen, TX 75013

Dear Sir or Madam,

I've just reviewed my credit report and have noticed there are several inaccurate items on my report. This is a summary of the disputed accounts.

CapitalOne Visa Acct: xxxxx-xxxxx-xxxx-xxx:
This account is listed as being 30 days late. I have never been late on this account.

Macys Acct: xxxxx-xxxxx-xxxx-xxx:

This account is listed as having a $3,980 balance. The balance has never been that high.

Best Buy Acct: xxxxx-xxxxx-xxxx-xxx: This account has been inactive for more than 7 years.

I have included a copy of my credit report with the disputed information highlighted.

In compliance with the Fair Credit Reporting Agency (FCRA), I request that you investigate this matter and update my credit report accordingly.

If your investigation validates the listing, please provide me with an explanation of the procedure you used to validate the listing within 15 business days of your completion of the investigation, as per the FCRA. I also request that you send me a copy of the information you gathered as a result of the investigation.

If your investigation shows this listing to erroneous, please update my credit report and send me a copy of my updated credit report.

Sincerely,

Your First and Last Name
Your Mailing Address
City, State Zip
Your Telephone Number
youremail@gmail.com
SSN: 000-00-0000

Enclosures: (List what you are enclosing.)

DISPUTING INACCURATE INFORMATION AND/OR ERRORS

March 25, 2019

Attn: Credit Report Disputes Experian
National Consumer Assistance Center
P.O. Box 2002 Allen, TX 75013

Dear Sir or Madam,

I am disputing some inaccurate information I have discovered on my credit report. The items I believe to be incorrect are listed below. I also include a copy of my credit report with the disputed information highlighted.

> **This is where you insert a summary of the items being disputed. It will include the creditors name, the account number, dates, amounts and any other information related to the account. You will find all this information in your credit report. Next to each, you will include the reason for the dispute.**

In compliance with the Fair Credit Reporting Agency (FCRA), I request that you investigate this matter and update my credit report accordingly.

If your investigation validates the listing, please provide me with an explanation of the procedure you used to validate the listing within 15 business days of your completion of the investigation, as per the FCRA. I also request that you send me a copy of the information you gathered as a result of the investigation.

If your investigation shows this listing to erroneous, please update my credit report and send me a copy of my updated credit report.
Sincerely,

Your First and Last Name
Your Mailing Address
City, State Zip
Your Telephone Number

youremail@gmail.com

SSN: 000-00-0000

Enclosures: (List what you are enclosing.)

DISPUTING NEGATIVE ITEMS AND/OR ERRORS

March 25, 2019

Attn: Credit Report Disputes Experian
National Consumer Assistance Center
P.O. Box 2002 Allen, TX 75013

Dear Sir or Madam,

I am writing to dispute the following information in my file. I have circled the items I dispute on the attached copy of the report I received.

These items include:

> **This is where you insert a summary of the items being disputed. It will include the creditors name, the account number, dates, amounts and any other information related to the account. You will find all this information in your credit report. Next to each, you will include the reason for the dispute.**

I am requesting that the item be accurately modified or removed entirely to correct the information. Please investigate these disputed items as soon as possible.

Sincerely,

Your First and Last Name
Your Mailing Address
City, State Zip
Your Telephone Number
youremail@gmail.com
 SSN: 000-00-0000

Enclosures: (List what you are enclosing.)

DISPUTING NEGATIVE ITEMS AND/OR ERRORS

January 15, 2018

Attn: Credit Report Disputes Experian
National Consumer Assistance Center
P.O. Box 2002 Allen, TX 75013

Dear Sir or Madam,

According to my rights under the Fair Credit Reporting Act, I am requesting that the following entries below be corrected, modified, or removed from my credit file. My file information is...

John D. Consumer 3737 Walnut Street
Raleigh, NC 27513
919-460-9628
jdconsumer@gmail.com
SSN: 452-56-9980
Date of Birth: 01/05/1982 Credit Report ID:

567-890A4

Credit Report Date: January 1, 2018

A summary of the entries to be removed or corrected include;

> **This is where you insert a summary of the items being disputed. It will include the creditors name, the account number, dates, amounts and any other information related to the account. You will find all this information in your credit report. Next to each, you will include the reason for the dispute.**

I also include a copy of my credit report with the disputed information highlighted. I am requesting that the items listed be accurately modified or removed entirely to correct the information. Please investigate these disputed items as soon as possible.

Sincerely,

Your First and Last Name
Your Mailing Address

City, State Zip

Your Telephone Number

youremail@gmail.com

SSN: 000-00-0000

Enclosures: (List what you are enclosing.)

DISPUTING ERRORS

March 25, 2019

Attn: Credit Report Disputes Experian
National Consumer Assistance Center
P.O. Box 2002 Allen, TX 75013

Dear Sir or Madam,

This letter is a formal request to correct inaccurate information contained in my credit file. The items listed below are completely (inaccurate, incorrect, incomplete, erroneous, misleading, outdated). I have enclosed a copy of the credit report your organization provided to me on January 3, 2014 and circled in red the item in question.

Per the federal Fair Credit Reporting Act (FCRA), I respectfully request you investigate my claim and, if after your investigation, you find my claim to be valid and accurate, I request that you immediately delete, update or correct the items.

> **This is where you insert a summary of the items being disputed. It will include the creditors name, the account number, dates, amounts and any other information related to the account. You will find all this information in your credit report. Next to each, you will include the reason for the dispute.**

If your investigation shows the information to be accurate, I respectfully request that you forward to me a description of the procedure used to determine the accuracy and completeness of the item in question within 15 days of the completion of your re-investigation as required by the Fair Credit Reporting Act.

I thank you for your consideration and cooperation. If you have any questions concerning this matter, I can be reached at the contact information listed below.

Sincerely,

Your First and Last Name

Your Mailing Address

City, State Zip

Your Telephone Number

youremail@gmail.com

SSN: 000-00-0000

Enclosures: (List what you are enclosing.)

DISPUTING NEGATIVE ITEMS AND/OR ERRORS

January 15, 2017

Attn: Credit Report Disputes Experian
National Consumer Assistance Center
P.O. Box 2002 Allen, TX 75013

Dear Sir or Madam,

This letter is a formal complaint that you are reporting inaccurate and incomplete credit information.

I am distressed that you have included the below information in my credit profile and have failed to maintain reasonable procedures in your operations to assure maximum possible accuracy in the credit reports you publish.

Credit reporting laws ensure that bureaus report only 100% accurate credit information.

Every step must be taken to ensure the information reported is completely accurate and correct.

I also include a copy of my credit report with the disputed information

Highlighted is a summary of the information which needs to be investigated immediately include.

> **This is where you insert a summary of the items being disputed. It will include the creditors name, the account number, dates, amounts and any other information related to the account. You will find all this information in your credit report. Next to each, you will include the reason for the dispute.**

Under federal law, you have 30 days to complete your reinvestigation. Be advised that the description of the procedure used to determine the accuracy and completeness of the information is hereby requested as well, to be provided within 15 days of the completion of your reinvestigation.

Sincerely

Your First and Last Name

Your Mailing Address

City, State Zip

Your Telephone Number

youremail@gmail.com

SSN: 000-00-0000

Enclosures: (List what you are enclosing.)

REMOVING INQUIRIES FROM YOUR CREDIT REPORT

Prepare letters to each inquiring creditor, asking them to remove their inquiry. The *Fair Credit Reporting Act* allows only authorized inquiries to appear on the consumer credit report. You must challenge whether the inquiring creditor had proper authorization to pull your credit file.

Your letter can go something like this:

Re: Unauthorized Credit Inquiry

Dear American Express,

I recently received a copy of my Experian credit report. The credit report showed a credit inquiry from your company that I do not recall authorizing. I understand that you shouldn't be allowed to put an inquiry on my file unless I have authorized it. Please have this inquiry removed from my credit file because it is making it very difficult for me to acquire credit.

I have sent this certified letter mail because I need your prompt response to this issue. Please be so kind as to forward me documentation that you have had the unauthorized inquiry removed. If you find that I am remiss, and you did have my authorization to inquire into my credit report, then please send me proof of this.

REQUESTING ORIGINAL CREDITOR TO INVESTIGATE A NEGATIVE LISTING

Date

Your Name
Your Address
City, State Zip

Credit Card Company
Credit Card Company Address
City, State Zip

Re: Acct #XXX-XXX-XXXXXXX

Dear Credit Card Company,

I recently pulled my credit report from Experian and TransUnion and, to my amazement, saw that you recently have decided to report me 30 days late on this account in (list the dates). I immediately disputed this information with Experian and TransUnion, and the results of the investigation came back "verified." Not only was I never late on this account, but according to the Fair Credit Reporting Act (FCRA), as the information furnisher, you are required to notify me of the insertion of negative listings.

Since I have disputed the late reporting's with the credit bureaus, and you obviously "verified" them, I am very curious as to what kinds of "records" you may have for this alleged account. Under the FCRA, you are required to investigate this account if I request it. I, therefore, am submitting my written request to you to investigate. Per the FCRA, you have 30 days to conduct this investigation and respond to my request. If you do not respond within this period, per the FCRA, you must remove this negative information.

Sincerely,

Your Signature

GOODWILL LETTER

This letter is a "Goodwill" letter requesting a creditor to remove a late payment or two because you have been a good customer. You are appealing to the creditor based on a good recent paying history.

You will need to alter this letter to fit your situation and late payment history. Please go through this letter carefully and make sure to edit it where needed.

Date
Your Name
Your Address

Creditor
Creditor Address

RE: Your Account Number

Dear "Creditor":

I have been a (creditor's name) customer since (date you opened the account), and during that time, I have enjoyed my experience with (the creditor) immensely. I am writing to see if you would be willing to make a "goodwill" adjustment to your reporting to the three credit agencies. I have a few late payments on the above-referenced accounts that date back to (insert dates). All but 1 of the late payments are 30-day late. Since that time, I have been an exceptional customer paying early every month and have been rewarded by (the creditor) with ever-increasing limits and lower APRs.

Because of my exceptional payment history over the last 3 years, I would like you to consider removing the negative payments from my credit report. At the time of those late payments, I was a full-time college student without a job. I say that not to justify why the payments were late, but rather to show that the late payments are not a good indicator of my actual creditworthiness. I hope that MBNA is willing to work with me on erasing these marks from my credit reports. I have been a very happy customer in the past and hope to continue a long relationship with (the creditor).

With today's credit industry so competitive, I know how important it is to maintain good relationships with customers. (Creditor) has been exceptional in my book so far, and I highly recommend it to all my friends and relatives. I hope that you will deeply consider my request and prove once again why (the creditor) is heads above the rest.

I look forward to your reply.

Sincerely,
Your Name

REDUCTION OF DEBT

The following is a sample letter requesting the reduction of a debt owed, and once signed, it is a binding contract for the settlement amount.

This letter is sent to a collection agency confirming an offer to settle a debt and the amount the debt was settled for. It is very important this type of settlement is in writing and signed by all parties involved.

AGREEMENT TO COMPROMISE DEBT

ABC Collections, Inc, referred to as COLLECTION AGENCY and John Q. Consumer, referred to as CONSUMER, agree to resolve the matter of the alleged debt, originally held by the _____ Company, hereafter referred to as the CLIENT. CONSUMER hereby agrees to settle this alleged debt claimed by COLLECTION AGENCY on the following terms and conditions:

The COLLECTION AGENCY certifies that it is legally authorized to act on behalf of its CLIENT and that any agreement that the COLLECTION AGENCY makes on behalf of the CLIENT is legally binding on the CLIENT. The COLLECTION AGENCY and the CONSUMER agree that alleged debt is $_____.00 (_____ & 00/100 dollars).

While the CONSUMER feels that the validity of the debt has not been proved by the COLLECTION AGENCY, the parties agree that the COLLECTION AGENCY shall accept the sum of $_____.00 (_____ & no/100 dollars) as full payment on the debt. The acceptance of the payment will serve as a complete discharge of all monies due, and the COLLECTION AGENCY agrees to consider the debt paid in full and agrees to not take further action to collect on the alleged debt. The payment shall be made in the form of a cashier's check or money order.

Upon payment of the $_____.00, the COLLECTION AGENCY agrees to remove any listing or information that the COLLECTION AGENCY may have placed on the CONSUMER'S credit report. The COLLECTION AGENCY agrees to never at any time in the future place any information on the CONSUMER'S credit report.

The CONSUMER feels that the negative information on CONSUMER's credit report is damaging, and while the exact estimation of the damage is not currently known, the CONSUMER estimates it to be $10,000 (ten thousand dollars and zero cents). Should the COLLECTION AGENCY fail to remove the listing or reinsert it later, the COLLECTION AGENCY agrees to award liquidated damages of $10,000 to CONSUMER. This compromise is expressly conditioned upon the payment being received by (date). If the CONSUMER fails to pay the compromised amount by (date), this contract will be immediately terminated.

The person signing this agreement,

_____,

hereby declares that he/she is authorized to act as an agent of the COLLECTION AGENCY.

This Agreement shall be binding upon and inure to the benefit of the parties, their successors, and assignees.

Dated:

Signature: _____
Legal Representative of ABC Collections, Inc.

Signature: _____
John Q. Consumer

DEBT VALIDATION LETTER - A SHORTER VERSION

You don't have to go quoting a bunch of laws and regulations the first time you request debt validation from a collection agency. Merely requesting them to validate the debt you owe, it is enough to start the ball rolling under the FDCPA.

Date

Your Name

Your Address

City, State Zip

Collection Agency

Collection Agency Address

City, State Zip

Re: Acct # XXXX-XXXX-XXXX-XXXX

To Whom It May Concern:

I just pulled a copy of my credit report and noticed that your agency is reporting that I owe you a debt.

I was not aware of this debt until now, and under my rights under the FDCPA, I request that you validate this debt.

Sincerely,
Your Signature

BONUS TIPS

PAY YOUR DEBT DOWN

If you are like most Americans, you have a sizable amount of debt already. How in the world will you be able to get your credit score up if you are struggling with a large pile of debt? The tips provided here should be a great place to start. The key is to work towards your debt step by step until you can pay it down totally. In other words, if you have a lot of debt, just start working towards paying it down now.

There are two main objectives to consider when paying down debt. Choose the method that works best for you.

1. Pay down your debt payments, making the minimum payments on all your accounts except for the one with the lowest amount owed. Pay this one with as much as you can until it is paid off. Then, take all the extra

you have (including the minimum payment from the first paid off account) and apply it towards the next lowest debt you have. Keep going one by one. The benefit here is that you are paying down your debt quickly: you will see results more often at first, which is great motivation to keep going.

2. Apply the same practice as in the last method, but this time, arrange your debts by the amount of interest that is charged on them, with the highest debt being paid off first. This way, you can pay down the type of debt that is costing you the most. Technically, you will pay less on the debt this way, too.

In either of these options, stop using your credit cards regularly. Put them away. Save them for a rainy day. Put away $1000 into a savings account for emergency needs. Use it just for emergencies. This keeps you from applying too much debt to your credit cards. Eventually, you cut your debts considerably.

PAY MORE THAN MINIMUM PAYMENTS

One of the mistakes many people make is to make payments on their accounts but only to make minimum payments. The minimum payment on your account is perhaps the worst payment to make besides no payment at all. Even paying a few extra dollars is better. Here is why.

If you pay just the minimum payment on a loan, any loan, you will likely pay that debt for years longer than you need to. On a credit card, borrowing just a few thousand dollars may mean only paying $50 a month to repay this debt. But that minimum payment is only a fraction larger than the finance charges for each month. You will remain in the loan ten, twenty, or even thirty years, depending on the amount of debt it is. For this reason, it is exceptionally important for individuals who are carrying debt month to month to pay off that debt as quickly as possible by paying more than the minimum payment.

Look at it another way. You may not have thought about paying extra per month on your mortgage payment, but this, too, can help you. For example, if you pay a few hundred dollars extra each month on your loan, or you may payments every other week rather than once a month, you could cut five to ten years off the loan's length. This also means a savings of hundreds of thousands of dollars in interest charges. Use a credit card calculator or mortgage calculator to figure out what you are really paying to borrow those funds and to pay it back so slowly!

PLANNING FOR A CREDIT-WORTHY FUTURE

Credit can be a fickle thing if when you don't understand it, many things can come about and bite you in the rear, leaving you with a credit mess. The best way to avoid those messes or recovery after coming out of a financial mess is to plan your financial future and set some boundaries for yourself for a better, more solid financial future.

Planning for your future can look like a lot of things and should involve many different aspects, like living within your means, things you want to accomplish financially, what you want out of your future credit, how you will build and maintain your credit and how you will set guidelines for yourself to avoid making common credit and financial mistakes. This chapter with touch briefly on each one of these to offer you more insight into how to plan for a credit-worthy future.

LIVING WITHIN YOUR MEANS

What does this mean exactly, well it means not spending more than what you make each month. This is one of the hardest and almost impossible things for American families to do, especially when your household expenses exceed their income. Ideally, you need to be able to pay all your bills on time each month and still be able to buy amenities like food and clothing, while sticking some in savings. To live within your means can be making choices between an upgraded cell phone plan and one that just covers what you mean. It can be the difference between eating out or learning to cook and staying in. There are lots of ways to shrink your monthly expenses to live more within your means.

What Do You Want to Accomplish Financially? This can accompany the living within your means, because if you are just distraught over the situation and want to have more luxuries in life, then you simply need to earn more money. You should look at the life you would like to live and then estimate what it would take months to make that life happen. You then would need to put together a plan to meet those needs before you start living that way. This could mean seeking out more training in your industry, asking for a raise, changing jobs, or taking a second job. The important thing is to always stay within your current means, even if you are looking for a way to increase your income. Until you are making that higher income, it is not available to you.

What Do You Want Out of Your Future Credit? Most will answer with buying a house, buy a car, vacations, college for the kids, and retirement. These are all great and should be goals depending on your family and personal situation, but all these things and those like them require decent to good credit and some planning to obtain securely. Think about the types of things you want in these areas and speak with professionals in the industries to see what it would look like on paper. This will give you a realistic sense of what it takes to get your credit to the point of being able to afford and finance the things you want.

Build and Maintain Your Credit
To build and maintain your credit, you need to stick with the guidelines surrounding the living within your means section, and that means paying your bills completely on time every time. This is not always possible but should be strived toward and if not met, should be made up as quickly as possible to get yourself back on track toward building and maintaining good credit.

Set Guidelines for Yourself
It's important to set some spending rules and good habits for yourself. Don't completely deprive yourself; this will only lead to failure and can have catastrophic results for your finances and future. Instead, set some ground rules with occasional indulgences and stick money aside in savings for the big rewards.

Smart money practices will always win out over excess in the long run.

LIVE THE LIFESTYLE YOU CAN AFFORD

Perhaps the most important bit of help available to you is this simple sentence. You need to live the type of lifestyle that you can afford, not one that is reliant on credit cards. The sad fact is that if you take away all the debt you had, you probably would have much more money per month to buy what you want and to live the way you want to. The key is not to have to pay the finance charges that often hurt the average consumer.

Determine what your lifestyle is by using a cash-only system for at least one month. For that entire month, do not make any type of charge to your credit cards. You will need to still pay them on time, including your mortgage loans. Instead of charging dining out or purchases to a credit card, only use cash. At first, you may find this very limiting, but imagine if you had all the money available to you that you are currently paying towards your debt each month. What you may find is that it is not only affordable to live on cash-only, but it may be a better lifestyle with less stress.

Making good decisions about credit is difficult to do for anyone. Yet, you can easily accomplish this by spending your time making good financial decisions overall. The process will allow you to walk away, finding yourself in a financially sound situation rather than a financially poor situation.

Use these ten tips to help you through the process of cleaning up your credit debt, not just today but going into the future, too.

USE CREDIT WISELY

Credit is like a gift. You get it, but only for as long as you take care of it. Stop taking care of the gift, and it will fall to pieces. It is much more difficult to pick up those pieces and tries to put the puzzle back together than just to maintain the gift in the first place.

Take credit seriously and only use it when you need to use it. For example, it is important to realize that credit that is used during the month should be paid off within the month. That way, you do not pay any financing charges, and your balance remains low.

It may be important to know what the credit reporting agencies think is important when it comes to credit reports:

- Low balances compared to the amount of available credit
- Payments are made on time
- You do not have too many credit cards
- The amount of total debt you have is not too high, or higher than what is considered appropriate for your income level. This is a debt to income ratio.

It is best to keep the credit you have low in use. Make your payments on time and be sure that you are monitoring your credit limits as often as possible. Paying off the balance on your credit cards on time is quite helpful to maintain a low balance and saving yourself a good deal of money in the process.

Credit is necessary for purchasing a home and buying a car, most of the time. You will need it throughout your life, which is why you will need to keep your long-term financial goals in mind when using credit for any reason.

DON'T OVER OBTAIN

Many times, it can seem like lenders are willing to give you an unlimited amount of credit. Beware of this. Lenders may see your credit report and believe you are a good risk. They may not realize that three, four, or more credit lenders have also noticed this and have offered you lines of credit. It is easy to get too much credit.

You may be thinking, "Is there such a thing as too much credit?" The answer to this is yes! If you have too much credit, lenders will begin to freeze up on you. The problem is the credit to income ratio or the amount of money you bring in with the amount of potential credit you have available to you. If you have too much credit, the lender may determine that you are too risky to lend more money to, even if you have a lot of open, available credit.

In this situation, you may not have a problem unless you are hoping to get a large loan such as a home loan or a home equity line of credit. In these situations, you may be limited.
Obtain only the amount of credit that you need to have. Even if you do get offers from a variety of other lenders over time, you do not have to get them all!

In situations where you receive an offer for a lower interest rate than the rate you are already paying, consider closing the original line of credit before accepting the new line of credit. If the account will close after you pay it off completely and it is not one of your oldest credit cards, you may find closing it to be an easy decision.

DO USE CREDIT

You are likely confused. Didn't we just say not to use credit but to pay down your debt? This is true and should be something that you spend a good deal of time doing. If you are carrying debt month to month, its likely costs you a great deal of money. Paying down your debt as much as possible is a must to get your credit score up. The problem you may encounter, though, is that once you have paid off that credit, you have no real credit history for the current period.

So, what do you need to do? Work to pay down your credit. If you are carrying debt month to month, pay it off as quickly as possible. You will want to maintain only lower balances whenever it is possible to do so.

Once you have it paid down to a level you feel comfortable about paying off within a month, use your credit again. However, there are some very strict guidelines to remember here:

1. Only make purchases you can pay off within the month. You want to get the bill and pay off the entire balance.

2. Know your grace period, or the amount of time you can borrow money without accruing any finance charges. Most lenders have a 25-day period between months that allows you to use the credit line and pay it off without incurring any finance costs.

3. Use credit only when you need to. Instead of making large purchases using credit, use it for those costs that you are confident you can repay each month. For example, you

may want to use a credit card for your gas purchases throughout the money, knowing you will have the funds to repay the debt. This allows you to accumulate no debt from month to month.

Credit card debt is not a good thing. Still, to have a good credit history, you will need to use credit from time to time. Show that you are a good credit risk by making payments on time each month to pay off the total amount of money you borrowed throughout the month.

BUILD CREDIT WITH SECURED CREDIT CARDS

Perhaps you already have bad credit. Cleaning up your credit card and removing any of the old, outdated information there should help. You may also see an improvement in your credit score if some of the creditors are unable to prove your obligation to pay the loan. Yet, even when you do clean up your credit report, the damage to it over this period can be harsh to your credit score. One way to boost it is to obtain new credit and work towards showing that you are a good risk by making payments on time and keeping your balance low.

Like all good catch 22's, though, to build credit means that you would have to have access to it. The good news is that there are options available for doing just that. These are called secured credit cards. Your goal is to find a credit card that's secured that also reports to credit agencies. Many now do this since it is far more attractive to the borrowing when it does.

A secured credit line is quite different from a standard line of credit. Here, the credit line you are given is based on the amount of cash you have paid towards the card in the form of a deposit. For example, you pay $1000 of a deposit and therefore have a $1000 credit line of credit to use. You'll use it and make payments on it as you do with a standard line of credit. The difference here is that your balance is there for "just in case" situations where you may default on the loan. The lender has protection from this.

At the same time, your good credit habits are also helping you to get a better credit score since the card is reporting each month to the credit agencies.

DEBT NEGOTIATION: NEGOTIATE AWAY YOUR MEDICAL DEBT

Medical debt affects millions of households around the country and can often be debilitating on the quality of life for those struggling to pay off medical debt while still managing the household and all the expenses of raising a family. There are ways to work around your medical debt that will pay off the debt as well as protect your credit rating and score. To find a way of dealing with medical debt before it goes into extreme financial consequences, like garnishments and collections, you should consider the possibilities of debt negotiation and other credit counseling services.

Debt negotiation is a form of debt management that allows you, or a representative for you, to negotiate with your medical creditors for a lower pay off amount, lower monthly payments, or lower interest rates. The art of debt negotiation can be learned, and you can take control of your own medical debt or if you feel unconfident about the process, there are credit counseling organizations that can negotiate your medical debts for you.

Before you start calling your medical creditors, you need to have a handle on all your medical debt to know how much you owe to whom and what the terms of the loan or account are. To know this, you need to make a list of your medical debts with the following information:

creditor, creditor contact information, amount of the debt, monthly payments, and interest rate. Highlight the interest rate and balance for each debt, these two items will be your main bargaining chips when you call.

There are a few key things to know before calling to negotiate your debt. You must speak with someone who is authorized to negotiate or make changes to your account. If you only speak to the first person who answers or a customer account representative, then you are wasting your time and potential negotiating power in the future. Specifically, ask for someone who can negotiate your account and wait until the right person is found. The best negotiation you can use is offering a lump sum payoff to pay the account off at a lower rate than the current balance. If you have money to work with, this is your best course of action and can work great with medical bills. While the creditor will be losing out on potential interest, they will be getting a guaranteed payment.

If you are unable to convince the creditor to take a settlement amount, the next best thing is to talk down the interest rate. This can save you hundreds, even thousands, off the life of the loan, depending on the amount and length of the initial loan. Both methods can be extremely powerful ways to handle medical debt and should be considered before taking a more extreme approach, like bankruptcy.

Your medical debt can be managed, and you can find a way to get out from under the suffocating medical debt you face. Debt negotiation is a great way to take control of the situation and not allow creditors to push you around while still respecting the role they play in the financial world and to your credit rating. Debt is an ugly four-letter word, but a reality in every household across the country and around the world. Don't be intimidated by your debt and be paralyzed by fear, instead find confidence and take control of the situation. You will find yourself on your way out from under medical debt and toward a brighter financial future.

DEBT NEGOTIATION: CUT YOUR SCHOOL LOANS IN HALF OR MORE

School loan debt can seem like a shock when you first graduate from school and find yourself not only starting a life and looking for a job but also faced with immediate and sometimes multiple payments toward all the money you borrowed during your academic career. If you drop out of school for any reason, you are also faced with the same dilemma, which can feel unjust and complicate whatever you are already going through. There are ways to deal with student loan debt that can be easy on your credit and help you get on your feet and start your financial life solid and successfully.

Debt negotiation is a form of debt management that allows you to work with your creditors and find an acceptable pay off the amount that can reflect good credit practices and satisfy the debt at the same time. Debt negotiation services are offered through many different types of financial businesses and institutions, but with a little help, you can learn to negotiate with creditors on your own and find success. Follow a few simple rules to negotiate away from your student loan debt and find relief from financial pressure.

1- Understand what debt negotiation is
It's important to know exactly what debt negotiation is to be successful when negotiating about your school loans. Debt negotiation is a way to talk with creditors and offer a settlement amount for less than the current balance to pay off the debt in full. This

is a controversial form of practice on the creditor's end as they lose out on all the interest you would have paid over the life of the loan, but they are guaranteed the money when in the future, you could default.

2- Look at your current loans
Make a list of all your current student loan debt with the following information for each: current balance, current monthly payment, interest rate, creditor, and creditor's contact information. The contact information is the most important thing to know because you want to make sure you are going to be able to speak with an actual person and not a call center employee or other individuals who are not authorized to speak with you. Also, the balance is your bargaining chip, so it's important to know what that balance is.

3- Talk to the right person
The key to successful debt negotiation is to make sure you are speaking with someone

who is authorized to negotiate with you about your account and can take a settlement offer. If you are speaking with someone other than a supervisor or account manager, then you are wasting your time and may not get anywhere with the creditor. When you are first intercepted by a live person, ask for a supervisor until you get someone who says they are authorized to negotiate a settlement offer with you.

4- Keep your options open

When negotiating with student loan creditors, you may hit a wall of resistance and find that they are not open to a settlement offer or lower the amount of the loan at all. Do not be completely discouraged and give up, instead refocus your attention and ask them to lower the interest rate, at least then if you must keep paying on a higher interest rate. This can shorten the length of your loan and reflect positively on your credit.

When you are looking for a way to get your school loans under control, don't discount some of the more strategic methods or worry that only an expert can handle them. Debt negotiation can come from anyone and is most credible when you, the account holder, are the ones trying to negotiate and work out a deal with the creditor. Obviously, a settlement amount and pay off are the best options to consider, but often you will not have a lump sum of money to negotiate with, so the next best thing is to work on the terms of your loan to make it work better for you.

DEBT NEGOTIATION: TALK DOWN YOUR CREDIT CARD DEBT

Credit card debt is the number one form of debt in the country, and every day more and more Americans are finding themselves in deeper and deeper with credit card companies. When the payments seem high and many, and the interest rates are beyond comprehension, you may be looking for relief. Debt negotiation can bring relief to the situation and allow you to fight for your hard-earned money and still make your creditors happy.

Debt negotiation is a form of debt management that allows for the debtor or a representative of the debtor to negotiate the terms of the loan with the credit card company to reach a settlement amount and form a payoff or reduce the interest rate, thus bringing relief to the debtor. What this means for you is a way to pay off your credit card balance while saving a little money or by bringing relief to your monthly payments and shortening the amount of time it takes to pay off your balance by decreasing the interest rate.

The first step to successful debt negotiation is to know as much as each of your credit card accounts as possible. Pull out all the information for each account you have a make a shortlist of the following information for each account to have readily available when you call. You need to have the account balance, monthly payment, interest rate, creditor, and full creditor contact information. Knowledge is power in this instance, and the more you know about the company and how the company compares to your other accounts, the better the negotiating power you have.

While, credit counselors are trained in the art of debt negotiation, and if you are unable to make the calls and negotiation yourself, you can find a credit counselor who offers debt negotiation services and have them make the calls for you. With that said, with a little courage and some confidence, you can negotiate your own account and contracts with great success and a few tips.

Tip #1: The most important thing to remember when negotiating with your creditors is that you MUST be speaking with someone authorized to make changes to your account. Otherwise, you are wasting your time. Only certain supervisors are authorized to offer settlements and make changes to accounts, and most people you talk to are only there for customer service and billing calls. Ask for a supervisor or account specialist before starting your pitch.

Tip #2: Put together some pay off the money and know your back up bargaining chips. The best thing you can do is offer a payout or settlement offer. To do this, you need a lump sum that you can pay them to settle the debt if they agree. If you are unable to offer this, then you need to have the information in front of you to negotiate other conditions like a lower interest rate. For this, you should have other credit card offers and accounts in front of you to offer what other companies are offering you. Many credit card companies would rather meet a lower interest rate than lose your business.

Tip #3: Don't take no for an answer. What this means is that if they don't go for a settlement or payout option, don't give up. Instead, ask for a lower interest rate or a loyalty credit to your balance. If they are resistant to lower your interest rate tell them, you have other offers that you have been considering transferring your balance to that offer a lower interest rate. They will often at least match it, if not beat it. Even if your account is the default, they would rather you stay with them and pay it than close the account and leave their company.

Debt negotiation can be a great tool for lowering your interest rates, monthly payments, or finding a way to pay off credit card debt. These tactics can all bring success when partnered with a confident attitude and understanding of the credit card industry. With a little work and negotiation, you can be well on your way to a life without credit card debt.

KNOW WHEN YOU NEED HELP

There will be times when you just cannot get out of debt on your own. You may find yourself struggling to make enough money to meet just the minimum payments, not to mention paying more than you owe. If you are struggling with your debt load, seek help. There is a variety of for-profit and not for profit options available to help you to get out of debt.

For your credit to improve, you need to get out of debt first. If you cannot do this on your own, the next best option is to secure the help of a professional who can work with you and your lenders to get the debt paid.

One option to consider is debt counseling. These professionals work with your lenders to get a lower monthly payment to reduce the amount of interest charged to you and sometimes to lower the amount you owe. You'll be on a monthly payment plan requiring you to make a set amount of payment each month. That single payment is divided by the counselor and paid to each of your lenders every month. Debt counseling can initially hurt your credit score, but over time, you will be paying down your debt and therefore find your way out of the debt hole. You may see your credit score increase because you are paying off the debt.

Bankruptcy is another option for some when all hope is lost in making monthly payments. Take it easy, though. Bankruptcy will put a black mark on your credit report for the next ten years! That is a long time to have a hurt credit score with no way to clean it off your report.

HOW TO SPOT A CREDIT REPAIR SCAM

Credit repair companies are all over the Internet and offered through other credit minded organizations, but can credit repair really be bought and sold, and do the practices used and promised really work? The short answer is no, but why? Instant credit repair, a new credit identity, and a chance to start over all sound amazing, but the reality is that just isn't the way credit works. Credit is built slowly over time as is the repair of financial mistakes made.

There are many credit repair organizations out there who offer to fix bad credit or boost good credit all for a fee. You could pay hundreds, even thousands, of dollars just to find out you've been victimized or to end up with worse credit. Most of these organizations are a fly-by-night operation that preys on those who are unknowledgeable or desperate about their current credit situation. When considering whether or not to use a credit repair or other credit, the organization must do an immense amount of research, and they should still be offering you something for nothing, instead of demanding a large upfront payment with no proof of what they claim to be doing. These fly-by-night companies will often have an exciting and energizing web site full of "testimonials" of people who have had success with them, but the testimonials are often fake and you will be hard-pressed to find any real information about the company, the people who run it or the level of expertise they have in the financial industry.

There is a fine line between credit counseling and credit repair. Credit counseling offers quality products and services designed to help you work to overcome your financial mistakes. These companies are often non-profit organizations or for-profit with extremely low or no fees for their services. They work to help you learn your mistakes and the proper ways to go about correcting, changing, or bouncing back from the negative reporting on your credit report. Credit repair organizations often claim to completely remove negative reporting, making the accounts and mistakes like they never existed, and that is just not possible.

It's important to remember that though it's impossible and illegal to just remove information from your credit report, you do have a right to dispute items that are incorrect or have not to be updated accordingly. This can be done through a dispute process, one of which each of the three major credit reporting agencies have, and companies have thirty days to respond to the dispute and either object or comply. Credit counseling agencies are designed to help you with this process and know the law, the Fair Credit Reporting Act, which surrounds this process. Credit removal or repair companies often do not know these regulations or try to convince you there are ways around it.

While, credit repair organizations have been around for years and some continue to get away with their unlawful, shady practices, the FTC (Federal Trade Commission) is on to them and has set up multiple investigations because of the high number of complaints by the consumers who have fallen victim to these companies. The FTC launched Project Credit Despair, which has been successful in capturing twenty so-called credit repair companies since its inception.

To avoid getting caught in a credit repair scam, there are distinct warning signs to watch for. These include companies that request payment before they provide the services. This is against proper credit practices, and a credible company will not ask for payment until the services have been completed. Companies must also inform you of your legal rights and tell you what action you can take yourself for free to help correct your incorrect credit reporting. They should never recommend for you to NOT contact credit reporting agencies directly you have this right and should use it. They may also recommend you start a new credit identity by applying for an EIN (Employer Identification Number) to use instead of your social security number. This is unlawful and an extremely bad idea. These are all red flags to watch for when trying to avoid a credit repair scam and should be reported immediately if you come across them.

Good credit is a privilege, not a right and you should learn how to earn good credit and correct inaccurate information, but the only true way to good, solid credit is to pay off your bills and plan for a better credit future by paying bills on time and only opening accounts you can pay off each month. Credit is extremely important, and regardless of what scam companies may tell you, you only have one credit report and score to work with.